There is no greater calling for [than the cultivation of Christlikeness in our lives and our outreach to others. The same was true for the earliest Methodists. In this volume Paul Chilcote skillfully and pastorally distills the wisdom that empowered and sustained them—and holds the same promise for today.

> —**Randy L. Maddox,** William Kellon Quick Emeritus Professor of Wesleyan and Methodist Studies, Duke Divinity School

Cultivating Christlikeness is a beautiful reflection and guide to embracing God's invitation to receive and share the love of Jesus Christ. Paul Chilcote offers deep, insightful, poignant wisdom grounded in a lifetime of practice and study that speaks directly to this season in the life of the United Methodist Church. This book is a rare—and timely—gift.

> —**Laceye C. Warner,** Associate Dean for Wesleyan Engagement, Duke University Divinity School

The Gospel is active faith. Visions must become ventures. Theology must be lived. The Wesleys knew this. So does Paul Chilcote, and in this book he leads us from the vision he cast in *Multiplying Love* to the enactment of it in Christlikeness. This is the practical divinity we so need in the church and world today.

> —**Steve Harper,** United Methodist Elder and Retired Professor of Spiritual Formation and Wesley Studies

In the midst of social turbulence, polarization, and struggle within and beyond the church, Paul Chilcote boldly writes that this is not a time for Christians to succumb to anxiety, but rather to lean in with "eager anticipation and joyful adventure." Chilcote skillfully weaves excerpts from Wesley's writing with helpful discussion and journal prompts, offering a beautiful resource to help readers trust the transforming and empowering work of Christ, "for such a time as this."

> —**Elaine Heath,** Abbess, The Community at Spring Forest

Paul Chilcote is an able guide for an immersive journey in what being, serving, and loving like Jesus Christ look like especially for Christian pilgrims walking the Wesleyan way. I look forward to gathering small groups around *Cultivating Christlikeness: Loving as Jesus Loved.*

> —**Gregory V. Palmer,** Bishop, The United Methodist Church

Cultivating Christlikeness

Cultivating Christlikeness

Loving as Jesus Loved

Paul W. Chilcote

Abingdon Press

Nashville

CULTIVATING CHRISTLIKENESS

ISBN: 9781791034788
Library of Congress Control Number: 2023944591

Originally published as *Wesley Speaks on Christian Vocation* (Nashville: Discipleship Ministries, 1987). Subsequently reissued by Wipf & Stock, Eugene OR, 2001, copyright © Paul W. Chilcote. *Cultivating Christlikeness* is adapted from this book and published by permission from Wipf & Stock.

Websites are accurate as of the date of publication.

MANUFACTURED IN THE UNITED STATES OF AMERICA

In honor of
Steve Harper,
my best friend

Contents

Acknowledgments

A friend is one of God's greatest gifts. I have been blessed to know Steve Harper for nearly fifty years. We first met at Duke University where he and I wrote our doctoral dissertations together under the direction of Frank Baker. We have shared some amazing adventures. Despite the physical distance that has separated us over most of these decades, we have retained a deep sense of connection. We are kindred spirits.

I owe this book to Steve. Some books are the product of your own imagination and vision. But sometimes other people open your eyes to a possibility you did not immediately see. Knowing my earlier book, *Wesley Speaks on Christian Vocation*, Steve simply said over a cup of coffee, "You need to rework this book for us today. It is exactly what we need." The rest is now history, as the saying goes.

I have dedicated this book, therefore, to Steve. You would not be holding it in your hands now, or reading it on a screen, without his insistence that I repurpose that book for a time such as this.

I shared this idea with Neil Alexander, and he was equally excited about resourcing the church with a book examining the central questions of our time. My thanks to him and to the team at Abingdon Press for picking up the idea and running with it. Paul Franklyn, who edited *Multiplying Love*, applied his skills to this book as well, and Marj Pon helped me navigate the production process to bring this to completion. I deeply appreciate their gifts and the gracious way they have supported and encouraged me.

Wipf & Stock released the rights to my earlier book, enabling this "new and improved" version to come to fruition seamlessly. My thanks to Charlie Collier and Jason Robeck in this regard.

My dear Janet always receives my final words of appreciation. No one who knows her will be surprised in the least when I say, "She is the most Christlike person I know."

The Backstory and
Forward Movement

Crises create unexpected opportunities. We know this is true in our personal lives. The same can be said of communities or institutions. Life seldom moves on a straight, upward trajectory. We have all experienced mountaintops and valleys. Both realities in life may have crises attached to them, but the valley—when you are in that deep dark place—can be traumatic. But I am convinced that God wastes nothing. God may not have caused the crisis; in my experience God seldom does. But God's Spirit can rush into any situation and nudge or push us into new discoveries, fresh experiences of grace, and even the vitality of abundant life.

Backstory

This resource for "a time such as this" repurposes an earlier book I wrote in relation to a community crisis. When I was a young United Methodist pastor, the resignation of our bishop plunged our conference into a dark place. We loved our bishop and were left abruptly without his presence or any way to mourn his loss properly. It was horrible. The morale of the entire conference was so low. It seemed as though things had fallen apart. Whatever vision of the future we had evaporated overnight. We were in crisis mode.

A number of senior clergy co-opted me into a small group to discuss what we might do to help one another through the journey ahead. We launched a movement called the Conference on Our Life Together. This response to the crisis became life-giving for many. We had two hopes. First, we yearned for healing. This gut punch had left everyone so breathless and depleted. We knew we needed to soak up God's presence and let the Spirit revive us. Secondly, we knew we all needed a renewed vision of our future. Many of us felt like we had lost our Moses. We needed to answer the question, Who are we now? Recovering our identity as we stepped into the future required a deep dive into our Wesleyan well. We knew intuitively that these waters would refresh us. We needed that refreshment if we had any hope of moving forward.

As a freshly minted PhD whose area of expertise was Wesleyan studies, my colleagues invited me to put together an appropriate resource to address these concerns. Discipleship Resources published *Wesley Speaks on Christian Vocation* the following year and pastors invited their churches to use it across the conference in small groups.

Forward Movement

Today we face a different kind of crisis. Polarization within the church, as well as society, has exhausted and depleted us. Many in The United Methodist Church feel battered, bruised, and bewildered. They feel like they've received a punch to the gut. Our grief is deep and real, and so is our disorientation related to competing claims about who we should be. We find ourselves in something of an identity crisis. We are asking the question, Who are we *now*? In moments like these, God delights in restoring God's people. God specializes in new birth and resurrection. In this current liminal space, amazing opportunity lies before us. We are now in a position to experience the healing balm of deep connection with one another. We can also rediscover who we are by exploring God's unique calling for the people called Methodists in our world today.

Sometimes children become our teachers in such things. On the last day of vacation Bible school, a little third-grader popped into my study to say good morning. I asked her if she was going to be in church on Sunday for our big celebration. Somewhat puzzled by my question she immediately replied, "Of course I'll be there! I'm baptized!" On Sunday morning, there she was in her usual place, with three neighborhood children who had never been to church before. She simply had to share her joy!

That little girl had a very clear understanding of who she was and to whom she belonged. No one could have illustrated Christ's promise to all and his claim upon his own more dramatically. In baptism she received a precious gift and assumed a challenging responsibility. She was in ministry. She was living out her true calling as a member of the Body of Christ. She had translated her experience of being loved and accepted into action. Empowered by God's grace, she was an agent for renewal, helping to make the community of God's new covenant a reality for others.

Vocation means calling. Christian vocation is our calling to new life in Christ. Christ calls us to become learners ("disciples") and gathers us into a pilgrim community to teach us how to love. Then he sends us out ("apostles") to serve the present age by sharing that love with others. We are called, not because of what we have done but because we are God's own people, formed by God's purpose and grace. Christlikeness is the goal of this dynamic adventure.

To be faithful witnesses in our own time we must ask penetrating questions about our life in Christ and our life together.

- Where can we see Christ at work in our lives? Our community? The world?
- What is Christ calling us to be and to do?
- How can peace and justice and love be experienced as realities in our common life?
- What does it mean to be part of the family of God?
- What is our calling at "a time such as this?"

We need to be in "connection" with one another to answer these questions. It takes a community to make a Methodist. We must engage in what the Wesleys called "conferencing." This requires listening as well as talking—opening ourselves to and embracing others rather than shutting them out. We need to celebrate our unity in Christ. Questions that address the whole family can only be fully answered when all of us engage them together. All this involves a process of discernment that moves us from believing to doing, from contemplation to action. We need to address these questions today more than ever. These questions lead to healing, discovery, and restored identity—to renewed vision and engagement in God's mission in the world.

John Wesley seems to have known all this intuitively. At the very first Methodist Conference in 1744 he encapsulated his own concerns about his time in three questions. Desperate to partner with the Spirit in the renewal of the church, he asked his preachers:

- What to teach.
- How to teach.
- What to do.

This is how he framed his response to the spiritual crisis of his own time by asking these questions. They can help us find our way today as well.

By addressing these three questions we posture ourselves in such a way for God to heal us and send us into the future restored and renewed. These questions continue to strike at the heart of our deepest needs in The United Methodist Church. This book repurposes *Wesley Speaks on Christian Vocation*—that earlier resource oriented around these three questions—for such a time as this. This need not be an anxious moment for us. It can be a time of eager anticipation and joyful adventure.

Using This Book

Answering the question about how to use this book begins with the title: *Cultivating Christlikeness: Loving as Jesus Loved.* If you are familiar with my earlier book—*Multiplying Love: A Vision for United Methodist Life Together*—you may have already noticed the parallelism in the titles. These books are companions. *Multiplying Love* is a "thought project" with serious implications about practice. *Cultivating Christlikeness* is a "practical guide" that helps us engage the questions so critical to our time. It elevates a high ideal, the idea that we can cultivate Christlikeness in ourselves and in our communities with God's grace and help. The goal of all things in the Wesleyan way is conformity to Christ in all things. This book provides a pattern by which to strive toward this goal—a rhythm of action and reflection, contemplation and action that revolves around conversations together.

Cultivating Christlikeness consists primarily of material compiled from the writings of John and Charles Wesley. Almost all these excerpts (with the exception of some hymns in particular) have been thoroughly modernized and occasionally abbreviated to make them more contemporary and energizing.

This book is designed primarily for use in small groups. Dialogue with others about what you are reading helps bring it to life. Each chapter is divided into three basic units. An introduction reflects briefly on the central question and the themes that emerge from it. Excerpts from the Wesleys' writings follow, with a collection of brief extracts followed by more substantial items that address the theme. Questions for thought and discussion, interspersed throughout the text, guide reflection and suggest ways in which to translate discoveries into action.

Hopefully, this book will find its way, therefore, into the hands of small group participants. Like *Wesley Speaks on Christian Vocation*, this book is designed as a resource to be used in small groups of four to seven members, like Covenant Discipleship Groups. We suggest that small groups such as these meet weekly or semi-weekly to discuss one chapter at a time in four sessions. Leadership in such groups can be shared by the participants, or a specific leader may be chosen by the group to guide them through the study.

This resource can be used effectively, as well, in church school classes, special study series, or can be incorporated into established Bible studies. This book might be particularly helpful for congregational leaders, especially in communities disrupted by disaffiliation or other difficulties. There may be United Methodists who seek connection with one another as they come out of disaffiliated congregations, seeking a new church home within United Methodism. This book avails itself well for online group use on zoom or other platformed gatherings.

While small group interaction around these questions adds depth and excitement about the learning, individuals can also use this book to great personal benefit. It can function as a manual for spiritual growth in the Wesleyan way. It invites every reader into a deeper love of God and others through practices that have been tested over time and define us as Methodists. For individual users, we recommend the practice of journaling. Keep a record of your thoughts and impressions throughout the course of your study. The questions interspersed throughout each chapter can be used as a guide for thoughtful written reflection.

Some readers, whether in groups or as individuals, may choose to study these materials devotionally throughout the course of the week. Others may prefer to stretch the reading out over the period of a month with a designated time for study each week. The preparatory seasons of the Christian Year are particularly suited for this kind of reflection. The four-week Advent season prior to Christmas and the five-week period in Lent prior to Palm/Passion Sunday are ideal. The lengthy season following Pentecost is an appropriate time to reflect on what it means to be a United Methodist engaged in God's mission in the world.

This book lends itself well to a retreat setting. For both individuals and groups, an overnight program of spiritual formation at a retreat center or church could prove to be a very meaningful experience. Here is a suggested program of study/reflection:

Day One	10:00am	Read Chapter 1
		Begin Journal Writing
	12:00noon	Lunch
	1:00pm	Read Chapter 2
		Meditation/Quiet Reflection
		Journal Writing
	4:00pm	Sacrificial Meal
	5:00pm	Read Chapter 3
		Meditation/Quiet Reflection
		Journal Writing
Day Two	7:00am	Breakfast
	8:00am	Read Chapter 4
		Meditation/Quiet Reflection
		Journal Writing
		Read The Character of a Methodist
	11:30am	Read/Celebrate Service of Covenant Renewal (umcdiscipleship.org/book-of-worship/covenant-renewal-service)

This book is for United Methodists who are eager to move forward into a future filled with the possibilities of love. God is at work for good in the world and seeks us to partner in this work with joyful abandon. We need to reclaim our inheritance. We have an unbelievably deep well out of which to draw living water. The age in which we live is crying out for empathy, authenticity, and integrity. This book is all about seeking to be like Jesus. This is the Wesleyan way and we can live into this again today. We seek for love to shine in our words and actions, to include everyone in our vision, and to grow into a more profound alleluia.

If we are sensitive and open, God will enable us to grow in Christian holiness and love. God will empower us to be faithful as a witnessing and serving community. As United Methodists we celebrate and seek to live into a grand vision of light and love that Charles Wesley helps us sing:

Christ, whose glory fills the skies,
    Christ, the true, the only light,
Sun of Righteousness, arise,
    Triumph o'er the shades of night;
Dayspring from on high, be near;
Daystar, in my heart appear.

Dark and cheerless is the morn
    Unaccompanied by thee;
Joyless is the day's return,
    Till thy mercy's beams I see;
Till they inward light impart,
Cheer my eyes and warm my heart.

Visit then this soul of mine;
    Pierce the gloom of sin, and grief;
Fill me, Radiancy divine,
    Scatter all my unbelief;
More and more thyself display,
Shining to the perfect day.

HSP (1740), 24-25

1

A Vision of a New Life Together

Introduction to a Refreshed Wesleyan Vision

John Wesley was a pilgrim and an explorer. Today we might call him a fresh expressions pioneer. He lived as though a life of gratitude was itself the greatest act of devotion. His spiritual journey was a quest for the fullness of God's love expressed in sacrificial love for others—Christlikeness. Charles Wesley, his brother and co-founder of Methodism, devoted his life to the creation of a poetry of love. His hymns, like *Love Divine, All Loves Excelling*, continue to shape our vision of life together with Christ.

The Wesleys were not alone in this pilgrimage of faith leading to deep love. They shared the journey with a host of faithful companions. They followed in the footsteps of a whole host of faithful disciples who pressed on toward the high goal to love God and neighbor. They never forgot about that great cloud of witnesses that surrounds us and cheers us on. Their story is captivating because it mirrors our quest for love in life together.

A great saint in the Church of England once described the essence of the Christian faith as an experience of the love of God in Christ changing our hopes and desires. No definition could better characterize the life of the Wesley brothers. They built their movement upon the foundation of a relational encounter with the God of love in Christ. They believed that this gift was a transforming friendship available to all. They discovered the freedom of living in the grace of God, and that discovery changed their lives and their world.

Today we live at a time in which we need to reclaim those discoveries for ourselves. In many ways the church has failed to communicate the love of God for every person effectively. In the early church, those outside the community of faith frequently declared, "My, how they love one another!" Unfortunately, people outside our communities do not see love in the church. Moreover, many have not felt love from the church. We need to open our hearts to a new transfusion of love into our common life.

In my earlier book, *Multiplying Love,* I make the claim that our world needs love during these desperate days of radical polarization and division. United Methodist churches yearn to embrace love more fully because God first loved us. I seek to provide guidance there to help us embrace anew the Wesleyan vision of Jesus as central to what we believe and how we live. While *Multiplying Love* includes some direction about how to live out God's vision, the central purpose of this book is to engage in conversation about this very thing—how to rediscover and enact God's vision of inclusive love.

We could find no better mentors in this quest for God's vision of love than John and Charles Wesley. They redirected people to a proper foundation for a life of faith working by love. They helped them discover that a sojourn through life with Christ is the greatest adventure of all. They provided means to nurture and empower their fellow pilgrims. Many of their discoveries can bring new life and excitement into our spiritual journey today.

In a recent *Oboedire* post my dear friend, Steve Harper, asks the question, How will the new United Methodist Church come to be? That is the kind of question we should always be asking because God never gives up on us and is always calling us onward and upward. That question never gets old because we are always "on the way," adapting to the new demands related to love that surround us day by day. In Steve's view, grace is the means, love is the message, connection is the method, and holiness is the mission of our becoming what God intends us to be. I could not agree more, and the vision we explore here reflects these values.

The Wesleys rediscovered the Bible as a place of divine-human encounter. They met and came to know the Living Word there. Saving faith nurtured in fellowship fanned the flame of love. Classic spiritual disciplines supported, nourished, and guided their companions on their way. Mutual accountability not only guarded them from dangerous diversions and divisions, but deepened their love for God and enriched their life of loving service to others.

In all this, the Wesleys' primary concern was for the realization of God's peaceable reign in the life of every beloved child of God and across the globe. Wherever they saw truth, they embraced it. They enabled their followers to discover their hidden potential and to fulfill their calling to be ambassadors of reconciliation and love. By enabling their co-workers and fellow pilgrims to grow in grace, they empowered them for partnership with God in God's mission.

Together they sought Christian wholeness. Their driving passion was to bring balance and vitality to the community of faith. We need a refreshed Wesleyan vision today.

Rediscovered Treasures

So who is God calling us to be today, and what is God calling us to do? If our response to that question is going to be Wesleyan in spirit, we must re-root ourselves in the transforming experience of God's grace. This comes through the embrace of Jesus Christ, realized through the power of the Holy Spirit. Our journey begins here.

Several foundational treasures emerge when we accept God's embrace and the unconditional love God offers to us all. First, the life of love is a precious *gift*. The most appropriate response to it is doxology—a life of unceasing prayer and praise. Second, God's *call* reorients and radically transforms us. Love only emerges from a life entrusted wholeheartedly to God's care, re-situated and energized by the power of love. Third, while the life of love has an intimate, personal character, it can only be realized fully as it is lived out in *community*.

Gift. Most of us have been raised on a steady diet of rugged individualism. Our tendency is to emphasize or value human potential and achievement rather than God's prevenient presence and initiative in our lives. But the lofty values I am writing about—grace, faith, hope, love—are all gift. We don't manufacture them. We don't possess them. They are gift, and love is the greatest gift of all. God empowers us both to receive and to perfect this gift.

Call. Like those ancient fishermen at their nets, we hear Jesus's call deep in our souls. Jesus does not call us simply to believe. He invites us to follow. So we are simultaneously those who entrust our lives to Christ (believers) and those who learn how to love from him

4

(disciples). Many churches today are filled with (but steadily losing) members who have never discovered the challenge and joy of discipleship. But the Spirit continues to call, to summon, to invite us all to enter a particular, revolutionary path of self-sacrificial love for the world. God's call is an invitation to participate in a new age of peace with justice—the rule of shalom.

Community. We need to be part of a community to build the courage it takes to enact the reckless abandonment of power and self that is central to our calling. This is utter foolishness in the eyes of the world. And so, those who believe are not only called out of darkness and death, but into fellowship with a crucified Lord. God gathers us together as a community of martyrs (literally witnesses). God links us to one another by means of a freedom that is bondage to love. The loving nature of our community becomes particularly visible in our solidarity with the least, the last, and the lost of the world.

The Wesleys offer profound insights in each of these areas. They believed that the Christian life is a way of devotion (*via devotio*). The classics of Christian spirituality taught them the importance of total consecration in the love of God and neighbor. They acknowledged the necessity of accountable discipleship in community. They understood how spiritual practices liberate the love we hold deep inside. Their movement of spiritual renewal was energized by personal encounter with Christ and shared Christian experience. We need to rediscover this transformational vision today. We need to embrace anew a way of spiritual devotion and a community of inclusive love.

Timeless Resources

The selections related to the rediscovery of true religion that follow remind us about the discoveries that fueled the Methodist movement of renewal. In correspondence, sermons, and theological writings, John Wesley elevates the centrality of love and restored relationships. Given their relational understanding of the faith, both Wesleys placed emphasis on the biblical concept of covenant. Their vision revolves around words like dedication, promise, gratitude, benevolence, sacrifice, happiness—covenant. Innovative practices, rules of life, and global vision gave fresh expression to the life of love.

"The Almost Christian," a sermon John Wesley preached at Oxford University, is the second of his so-called standard sermons. When he ascended the pulpit of St. Mary's Church on July 25, 1741 to preach this controversial sermon, the revival under his leadership was a fresh movement of the Spirit. The central theme of this manifesto is the radical difference between nominal and real Christians—between those who are members and those who have become disciples of Jesus. He contrasts the "almost" with the "altogether Christian." Both are in the household of God; the former, however, is a servant while the latter has discovered the joy of being God's beloved child.

John Wesley's sermon "On God's Vineyard" was published toward the end of his life in 1788. The aged evangelist assesses the Methodist movement after fifty years. He recalls the origins and essentials of a powerful religious awakening. His intention was patently personal and practical. He wanted the Methodist people to rediscover a vision of life together. He celebrates the fresh wind blowing across the church at the outset of his ministry. He wants his beloved followers to remember who they are. We need that same reminder today. Wesley calls us through this sermon to celebrate our identity and our calling.

SELECTIONS ON THE REDISCOVERY
OF TRUE RELIGION

True Religion

I take religion to be, not the bare saying over so many prayers morning and evening, in public or in private—not anything superadded now and then to a careless or worldly life—but a constant ruling habit of soul, a renewal of our minds in the image of God, a recovery of the divine likeness, an increasing conformity of heart and life to the pattern of our most holy Redeemer.

Works 25:369

What religion do I preach? The religion of love—the law of kindness brought to light by the gospel. What is this good for? To make all who receive it enjoy God and themselves, to make them, like God, lovers of all, contented in their lives and crying out at their death in calm assurance, "Where is your victory, Death? Where is your sting, Death? Thanks be to God, who gives us this victory through our Lord Jesus Christ!"

Works 11:51

It is in consequence of our knowing God loves us that we love God and love our neighbor as ourselves. Gratitude toward our Creator cannot but produce benevolence to our fellow creatures. The love of Christ constrains us, not only to be harmless—to do no ill to our neighbor—but to be useful and patterns of true genuine morality, of justice, mercy, and truth. This is religion and this is happiness, the happiness for which we were made.

Works 4:66-67

Does Wesley's definition of "true religion"
ring true for you, and if it does, what
are you doing in your daily life to
spread "happiness" in your world?

Covenantal Love

I resolved to dedicate all my life to God, all my thoughts and words and actions, being thoroughly convinced there was no medium, but that every part of my life (not some only) must either be a sacrifice to God or myself. I was convinced more than ever of the absolute impossibility of being half a Christian. And I determined, through God's grace (the absolute necessity of which I was deeply sensible of), to be all-devoted to God—to give God all my soul, my body, and my substance.

Christian Perfection, 33

I am no longer my own, but thine. Put me to what thou wilt, rank me with whom thou wilt. Put me to doing, put me to suffering. Let me be employed by thee or laid aside for thee, exalted for thee or brought low for thee. Let me be full, let me be empty. Let me have all things, let me have nothing. I freely and heartily yield all things to thy pleasure and disposal. And now, O glorious and blessed God,

Father, Son, and Holy Spirit, thou art mine, and I am thine. So be it. And the covenant which I have made on earth, let it be ratified in heaven. Amen.

UMH, 607

Come, let us use the grace divine,
    And all with one accord,
In a perpetual covenant join
    Ourselves to Christ our Lord;
Give up ourselves through Jesus' power,
    His name to glorify;
And promise, in this sacred hour,
    For God to live and die.

The covenant we this moment make
    Be ever kept in mind!
We will no more our God forsake,
    Or cast his words behind.
We never will throw off the fear
    Of God who hears our vow;
And if thou art well pleased to hear,
    Come down and meet us now!

Scripture Hymns, 2:36-37

**How would you describe the nature of your
commitment to God in your life, and how do
you maintain your level of commitment?**

9

A Fresh Expression

I could scarce reconcile myself at first to this strange way of preaching in the fields, of which Whitefield set me an example on Sunday, having been all my life (till very lately) so tenacious of every point relating to decency and order that I should have thought the saving of souls almost a sin if it had not been done in a church.

April 1. In the evening, Mr. Whitefield being gone, I began expounding our Lord's Sermon on the Mount (one pretty remarkable precedent of field preaching, though I suppose there were churches at that time also) to a little society which was accustomed to meet once or twice a week in Nicholas Street.

Mon. 2. At four in the afternoon I submitted to "be more vile," and proclaimed in the highways the glad tidings of salvation, speaking from a hillside adjoining to the city to about three hundred people. The scripture on which I spoke was this (is it possible anyone should be ignorant that it is fulfilled in every true minister of Christ?): "The Spirit of the Lord is upon me, because the Lord has anointed me. He has sent me to preach good news to the poor, to proclaim release to the prisoners and recovery of sight to the blind, to liberate the oppressed, and to proclaim the year of the Lord's favor."

Works, 19:46

A Methodist society is no other than a company of persons having the form and seeking the power of godliness, united in order to pray together, to receive the word of exhortation, and to watch over one another in love, that they may help each other to work out their salvation.

There is only one condition required of those who desire admission into these societies: a desire to flee from the wrath to come, and to be saved from their sins. But wherever this is really fixed in the soul it will be shown by its fruits.

It is therefore expected of all who continue therein that they should continue to evidence their desire of salvation,

First, by doing no harm, by avoiding evil of every kind.

Secondly, by doing good; by being merciful and, as they have opportunity, doing good of every possible sort, and, as far as possible, to all people.

Thirdly, by attending upon all the ordinances of God. These include the public worship of God, the ministry of the Word, either read or expounded, the Supper of the Lord, family and private prayer, searching the scriptures, and fasting or abstinence.

These are the General Rules of our societies, all of which we are taught to observe in God's Word which is the only sufficient rule both of our faith and practice. God's Spirit writes all these on truly awakened hearts.

Works, 9:69-73

All praise to our redeeming Lord,
    Who joins us by his grace,
And bids us, each to each restored,
    Together seek his face.
He bids us build each other up;
    And, gathered into one,
To our high calling's glorious hope
    We hand in hand go on.

The gift which he on one bestows,
  We all delight to prove,
The grace through every vessel flows
  In purest streams of love.
E'en now we speak and think the same,
  And cordially agree,
Concentered all, through Jesus' name,
  In perfect harmony.

Redemption Hymns, 43

I look upon all the world as my parish. Thus far I mean that, in whatever part of it I am, I judge it meet, right, and my bounden duty to declare unto all that are willing to hear the glad tidings of salvation. This is the work which I know God has called me to. And I am sure that God's blessing attends it. Great encouragement have I therefore to be faithful in fulfilling the work God has given me to do. I am God's servant and as such am employed (glory be to God) day and night in God's service. I am employed according to the plain direction of God's Word, "So then, let's work for the good of all whenever we have an opportunity." And God's providence clearly concurs with his Word.

Works 25:615-16

Redeemed by your almighty grace,
  I taste my glorious liberty,
With open arms the world embrace,
  While holding those embracing me;
I always in your saints delight,
Who walk with God in purest white.

Joined to the hidden church unknown
    In this sure bond of perfectness;
Obscurely safe, I dwell alone
    And glory in th'uniting grace,
To me, to each believer given,
To all your saints in earth and heaven.

Catholic Love, 30

**With regard to the "three general
rules," how would you define your
strengths and your weaknesses?**

The Almost Christian

Are you so quickly persuading me to become a Christian?
(Acts 26:28 NRSVUE)

1. Ever since the coming of Christ into the world, there have
been many in every age and nation who were almost persuaded to be
Christians. It is important for each of us to consider what it means to
be almost a Christian and what it means to be altogether Christian.

Characteristics of the Almost Christian

2. Those who are almost Christian are characterized, first, by
their honesty. They obey the rules that are commonly expected of one
another. They are not unjust. They do not steal from their neighbors.

13

They do not oppress the poor. Indeed, there is a sort of love and assistance which they expect from one another. And this may even extend into their feeding the hungry if they have food to spare, clothing the naked with their own superfluous clothing, and giving to any that are in need so long as they have no need themselves.

3. A second thing implied in being almost Christian is having a form of godliness—having the appearances of a real Christian. They obey the ten commandments. They may even go beyond the letter of the law in doing good to others. They reprove the wicked, instruct the ignorant, confirm the wavering, encourage the good, and comfort those who are afflicted in any way.

4. Those who have the form of godliness also use the means of grace. They attend worship regularly. They are serious and attentive in every part of the worship service. Whenever they received the Lord's Supper, everything in their behavior would seem to say: "God be merciful to me a sinner." They have daily prayers in their homes, and they set special times apart for devotions and meditation on the things of God.

5. In addition to all this, the almost Christian is also sincere. By sincerity I mean a real, inward principle of religion out of which these actions flow. The almost Christian is not moved to any of these actions by the fear of being punished, but truly desires to follow God. There is a real desire to serve God, a hearty desire to do God's will. And this motive runs through the whole tenor of life. It is the moving principle for doing good, abstaining from evil, and engaging in the means of grace.

6. I speak to you all very boldly. And I do so because this was the character of my life for many years as many of your know. I avoided all evil so I would have a clear conscience. I used every opportunity I

had to do good to everyone. I was devout both in public and private prayer, in the study of scripture, and in receiving Holy Communion. And I did all this with sincerity. My design was to serve God, to do God's will in all things, to please God who had called me to fight the good fight, and to win eternal life for myself. Yet in all this, I was an almost Christian.

**In which areas of your life do you still
feel like an "almost Christian" and
what do you need to do about it?**

The Altogether Christian

7. The first thing implied in being altogether Christian is the love of God. The Bible says: "Love the Lord your God with all your heart and with all your soul and with all your mind and with all your strength." This kind of love captures the whole heart, takes up all the affections, fills the entire capacity of the soul, and uses every gift to its fullest extent. The heart of this disciple continually cries out, "My Lord and my God. What else do I have in heaven but you? Since I have you, what else could I want on earth?"

8. Secondly, altogether Christians love their neighbor. If anyone asks, "Who is my neighbor?" we reply, "Every person who is in the world; every child of God." Neither can we exclude our enemies or the enemies of God. But every Christian loves these as Christ has loved us. Whoever would more fully understand what kind of love this is may consider St. Paul's description of it in 1 Corinthians 13.

9. One thing remains to be considered, namely, the foundation of these dual loves of God and neighbor. The ground of all—what

makes this kind of love possible—is faith. Faith is the keynote of scripture. Whoever believes that Jesus is the Messiah is a child of God. Faith gives the all God's children victory over the world. Jesus himself declares that whoever believes in him will not die but have eternal life. Indeed, these have already passed from death to life.

10. But do not be deceived. The faith of which I speak is living faith. It is a faith that works by love. The right, true, and living faith not only believe that the Bible and the creeds of the church are true; they also have a sure trust and confidence in salvation through Christ. Living faith is the sure trust and confidence that Christ died for me and saved me from the law of sin and death.

11. This faith purifies the heart by the power of God who dwells in us. It fills the heart with love stronger than death—a love both to God and to all humankind. Whoever has received this love rejoices in giving their whole life in the service of others. Whoever has this faith which works by love is not almost only, but altogether Christian.

**If love is the goal, what are the areas of your life
that require more of your work and more of God's
grace for you to be as fully loving as possible?**

A Practical Application

12. But who are the living witnesses of these things? I pray that each of you ask in the depths of your hearts: "Am I among their number of these altogether Christians? Am I just, merciful, and honest? If so, do I have the appearance of a Christian? The form of godliness? Do I avoid evil, pursue good, and immerse myself in the means

of grace God affords me? Do I have a sincere desire to please God in all of this?"

13. Perhaps you have not even come this far. Perhaps you are not even almost Christian? But if you have, do good designs and sincerity make a Christian? Someone has said that the way to hell is paved with good intentions. The greatest question of all still remains: Has the love of God been poured out in your heart? Can you cry out, "My Lord and my all?" Do you desire nothing but God? Are you happy in God? Is God your glory, your delight, your crown of rejoicing?

14. And is this commandment written on your heart: "Those who claim to love God ought to love their brother and sister also." Do you love your neighbor as yourself? Do you love every person, even your enemies, even the enemies of God, as your own soul? As Christ loved you! Do you believe that Christ died for you and gave himself for you? Do you believe that the Lamb of God has taken away your sins? Does the Spirit bear witness with your spirit that you are a child of God?

15. "Wake up, sleeper! Get up from the dead, and Christ will shine on you." Don't let anyone persuade you to rest short of the prize of your high calling in Christ Jesus. But cry to him day and night until you know in whom you have believed and can say, "My Lord and my God." Always pray and never be discouraged. You will one day be able to lift up your hands to heaven and declare to the One who lives for ever and ever, "Lord, you know everything; you know I love you."

16. May we all come to experience what it is to be not almost only, but altogether Christian! Being pardoned and relieved of the burden of sin freely by God's grace through redemption in Jesus,

knowing we have peace with God, rejoicing in hope of the glory of God, and having the love of God poured into our hearts by the Holy Spirit, who is God's gift to us!

17. Go out into the world, then, as a little child who believes in Jesus Christ. Though you are helpless and as vulnerable as an infant, the strongest enemy will not be able to triumph over your love. Now thanks be to God who gives us the victory through our Lord, Jesus Christ, to whom, with the Father and the Holy Spirit, be blessing and glory, wisdom and thanksgiving, honor and power and might, for ever and ever! Amen.

Works 1:131-41

What practical actions can you take today to live into the adventure that God lays before us?

⚬━━━◆━━━⚬

ON GOD'S VINEYARD

What more was there to do for my vineyard
that I haven't done for it?
When I expected it to grow good grapes,
why did it grow rotten grapes (Isaiah 5:4)?

1. The vineyard of the Lord, taking the word in its widest sense, includes the whole world. In a narrower sense it means the Christian world or all that name the name of Christ. In a still narrower sense it may be understood as the Protestant branch of the church. And in the narrowest sense of all, it may refer to the Methodist people.

2. What more could God have done in this vineyard? What insight did God provide for them in matters of doctrine? What aids did God provide for their spiritual growth? What forms of discipline made them strong? What kind of fruit was produced from all these efforts?

Doctrine

3. You could say that the Methodist movement began when several Oxford University students and tutors joined together to find ways of enriching their walk with Christ. Each of these men determined that he would be a man of one book, namely, the Bible. The Word of God became their only rule of faith and of practice. It guided the way they lived out their faith day by day.

4. Disciplined study of scripture and the Christian classics led these earnest seekers after truth to a clearer understanding of the faith. They discovered, for instance, that growth in grace was insep- arable from the experience of forgiveness—that faith and holiness belong together. They believed that the goal of life, which is nothing less than love of God and neighbor as Christ loved us, is directly related to where our journey starts in God's pardon and love. While faith is the means, love is the end of our life in Christ. Balance char- acterized their walk.

5. They were as tenacious about inward holiness as any mystic, and of outward holiness as any spiritual zealot. They believed that motives and actions ought to be consistent. There must be a correla- tion between one's personal experience of God's love in the depths of one's heart and the expression of that love in the ongoing relation- ships of life. Who then is a Christian according to the light that God has given to this people? A Christian is anyone who, being justified by faith has peace with God through our Lord, Jesus Christ.

"They were as tenacious about inward holiness
as any mystic, and of outward holiness as any
spiritual zealot." What does this statement mean
to you and where are you in relation to it?

Spiritual Growth

6. Two young clergymen [John and Charles Wesley], not very remarkable in any way, began to call sinners to repentance. The fruit of their preaching quickly appeared. Many sinners were changed both in heart and lie. These clergy had no plan at all. They only went wherever they had a prospect of saving souls. More and more people began to ask, "What must we do to be saved?"

7. Those who responded to their message of God's free grace for all people were divided into spiritual formation groups, or classes, according to where they lived. They appointed one person in each class to meet with all the rest on a weekly basis. In these small groups, the members became accountable to one another and assisted one another in their mutual endeavor to grow in grace. At that time, few communities had such a system of mutual accountability.

8. In order to increase the sense of unity among the preachers who cared for these expanding groups, they all met together for a special conference in London in 1744. They spent a few days considering what might be done for the good of the movement. Soon they found that what Paul observes about the whole church may be applied to every part:

The whole body grows from him, as it is joined and held together by all the supporting ligaments. The body makes itself grow in that it builds itself up with love as each one does its part (Ephesians 4:16).

9. God's whole design in raising up the people called Methodists was to spread scriptural holiness throughout the land. People of other denominations are allowed to hold their own opinions and to follow their own mode of worship. For the primary aim of the Methodist people has always been to renew the life of the world by proclaiming and living the message of faith working by love.

Are you currently participating in a small group? If yes, how has this been helpful with regard to your spiritual growth? If no, what impediments stand in the way of this kind of fellowship?

Spiritual Practices

10. The Methodists are especially noted for their spiritual practices. Nothing could be simpler, nothing more reasonable, than their system of caring for one another. It is entirely founded on common sense, particularly applying the general rules of scripture. Any person who wants to flourish spiritually is more than welcome to join them. But evidence of this desire must be demonstrated in three ways:

1. In their desire to do no harm to others,
2. In their efforts to do good according to their ability, and
3. In their participation in means of grace like prayer, scripture study, and Holy Communion.

11. Their public services of worship are at five in the morning, and six or seven in the evening. On Sunday they avoid conflict with their local parish churches by gathering at a later time, concluding their services with a celebration of the Lord's Supper. On Sunday evening the entire society (as it is called) meets for fellowship and instruction. The Methodist preachers evaluate the spiritual health of their members regularly. If any are defiant or deficient in terms of fulfilling their commitments, they are quietly and inoffensively removed, but with hopes of their return.

**What is your normal pattern of worship and
how do you find it to be spiritually energizing?**

The Consequence of Success

12. Every opinion, right or wrong, has been tolerated in almost every age. Every mode of worship has been tolerated, however superstitious or absurd. But true, vital, scriptural Christianity has never been tolerated. The Methodists have abundant reason to praise God for the way in which earlier persecutions have died away. But the general acceptance of the revival has affected the movement in negative ways.

13. At the beginning of the Methodist revival, so many people came to life in their first love. They magnified the Lord and rejoiced in God their Savior. One would have expected them to live like angels. One would have hoped for them to walk continually as if seeing and having constant communion with God. Living in eternity and walking in eternity, why would anything have changed?

14. But instead of this, success produced wild grapes. Particularly among those who became wealthy as a result of their faithful

stewardship, "success" produced the grand poison of the soul—the love of the world. O you that are rich in possessions, once more hear the Word of the Lord! You that are rich in this world, that have food to eat and clothing to wear, and much more than you need, are you safe from the curse of loving the world?

15. Are you aware of the danger? Do you realize how hard it is for those who have riches to enter the realm of God! When you sit down to lavish meals daily while others are hungry, do you realize how far this is from God's way? When you have to have the best, or the newest, and give no consideration to those who have nothing, do you not understand how far you have come from God's vision of enough for all. Are you not laying up treasure on earth instead of restoring to God in the poor, not a little here or there, but all you can spare? Surely it is easier for a camel to go through the eye of a needle than for a rich person to enter into God's realm of justice and peace.

16. The whole Word of God has been proclaimed to you. The foundational doctrines of God's pardoning love for you in Christ and of God's desire to restore Christ's image in you fully through the power of the Holy Spirit have been preached repeatedly to you. Every aspect of both inward and outward holiness has been explained to you and applied directly to your lives.

17. Could it be that your falling away was caused by your failure to join together in fellowship with other disciples of Christ? No one can be warm alone. Woe to those who are alone when they fall. Are your friends seekers after God? Do they encourage you to seek justice, and mercy, and peace? Do you have companions who watch over your soul as people who must give account? Do you have enough friends who freely and faithfully warn you if you take a false step or are in danger of doing so?

18. When you meet together in the name of the Lord, do you expect Christ to be in the midst of you? Are you thankful to the giver of every good gift for the general spread of true religion? Surely, you can never praise God enough for all these blessings, so plentifully showered down upon you, until you praise the Lord with angels and archangels and all the company of heaven!

Works 3:502-17

**Do you feel as though you are affluent,
and how has your affluence hampered the
development of a rich faith in God?**

2

What to Teach

Introduction to Wesleyan Practical Theology

The words "theology" and "doctrine" have a sleep-inducing tone for many people. Bogie Dunn, beloved founding Dean of the Methodist Theological School in Ohio, told me an interesting story related to this issue. He said that before he retired, when people asked him what he did for a living, he would say he was a theologian. As soon as the words were out of his mouth, he could see their eyes glaze over. Their interest and engagement evaporated immediately. After he retired, Bogie said he flipped the narrative. When asked what he did, he said he helps people find their way home. Their interest peaked immediately. He said he tries to connect people with what really matters in life. He did all he could to help them realize just how much they are loved and how thrilling it is to share that love with others. He was a good Wesleyan—a "practical theologian."

25

Some people outside Methodist circles caricature us as having no theology. They are sadly mistaken, but it depends on what we mean by theology and how we conceive its purpose. As Methodists we have inherited the Wesleyan understanding of theology as transformation. John and Charles believed that God changes us through our reflection on and conversations about big questions. John was a powerful preacher. But most of the early Methodist people were "converted," not under his preaching, but in the context of small group fellowship. In the intimacy of the Methodist bands and classes, they plumbed the depths of important questions about faith and life. They were all "dialogical theologians."

The Wesleys' practical theology was about transformation, not the mastery of dogmatic truths. They wanted their followers to embody the good news of God's love, not memorize timeless principles about it. They sought to cultivate the mind of Christ among those for whom real life sparks engagement and reflection. They refused to separate theology from spirituality. They held faith and practice together in a way that engaged the whole person—mind, heart, and will. Perhaps most importantly, the Wesleys sang their theology in community with other Christians. Using Charles Wesley's hymns, they expressed both words to and words about God. They were all "lyrical theologians" of God's unbounded love. Their goal was Christlikeness, not adherence to dogma.

Far from boring, or irrelevant, or esoteric, this practical theology brought people to life. It inspired them, challenged them, and called them onward and upward to their true purpose in life. Little wonder that the Wesleys modeled this whole approach to the integration of theology and life in their very first Conference. The structure itself reflected their way of doing theology as discernment around big, life-orienting questions. They engaged their preachers in conversation, first, about "what to teach." Doctrine was important to the Wesleys, and they had very clear ideas about what they believed, but the process of engaging this question was the purpose of their gathering. We call this "holy conferencing."

For the expanding movement to thrive and endure, John Wesley realized that the seed of faith had to be planted in rich and carefully cultivated soil. He knew that the Methodist people were called to be a clear but fresh expression of God's vision for a new age. For him, worship, doctrine, and life were integrally connected. He intuited the importance of self-understanding and faithfulness. He considered action and reflection to be essential to the vision he embraced. The vitality of early Methodism was contagious, in part, because Wesley encouraged his followers to struggle with the deep questions of life and talk about their experience of God.

We need to rediscover today what it means to engage in conversation about important questions related to faith-in-life. One of the most critical tasks before us is the discernment of God's vision within the context of God's family. God is also calling us today to connect our personal faith with a dynamic social witness as we partner with God in God's mission in the world. Three questions related to each of these areas of life surface immediately, and all of them bear on the larger question about what to teach:

- What is the heart of the gospel?
- What is the way of salvation?
- What is the goal of life in Christ?

The Heart of the Gospel

The Body of Christ is like a richly textured and variously colored mosaic. Each particular facet within the pattern, by retaining its own unique features and dimensions, is essential to the beauty of the whole. Likewise, the continuing United Methodist family is a richly diverse community of faith. We affirm our unity-in-diversity. Maintaining the integrity of this dynamic tension, however, requires vigilance and great love. Unity without diversity is stale uniformity; variety devoid of a unifying center can lead to chaos.

All this begs that larger question, What is the heart of the gospel? What is the central proclamation (*kerygma*) around which community (*koinonia*) can be built and out of which service (*diakonia*) can extend? By engaging in conversation with one another we rediscover who we are and what we believe God is calling us to be and to do. We are not just now launching this conversation. It has been ongoing for generations, beginning long before the birth of the Methodist movement. So we need to listen to the voices of the past—like those of John and Charles Wesley—as well as to those in this present moment. Spiritual discernment about God's mission of love and our place in it begins with dialogue and holy conferencing.

The Way of Salvation

The perennial question—What must I do to be saved?—stands at the heart of this quest. The British Methodists summarize the Wesleyan vision in what they call the "Four Alls." All people need to be saved. All people can be saved. All people can know they are saved. All people can be saved to the uttermost. They have packed a lot in those four statements. That vision necessarily shapes every aspect of who we are and what we do. It reveals our basic attitudes toward life, in all its tragic and triumphant dimensions. Some people approach this question of salvation from a narcissistic perspective. But the Wesleyan way teaches us to abandon self-interest. Rather than asking What am I saved from? it asks What are we saved for? It doesn't view salvation as a ticket to heaven; rather, it views redemption as enlistment in God's way of shalom.

Today we need to rediscover the transforming power of God's grace and love. We need a renewed understanding of faith in Christ as God's great gift to us. For this to happen, we must first be honest about our need and then enter the drama of God's restoring love. The Wesleys' ultimate concern was the discovery of living, saving faith, a faith made effective through love. John Wesley's preaching can be summarized in one word—"now." Charles's hymns can be summarized in one word—"love." They proclaimed and sang an urgency concerning God's love, because love was the origin, the journey, and the goal of all life. The Wesleys taught that trust (faith) in the God of love leads to Christlikeness—the fullest possible love of God and neighbor.

The Goal of Life in Christ

The Wesleys believed that those who had been captured by the love of God could not help but offer that love freely to others. Following the model of Christ, a heart filled with love expands to take the world into its embrace. They used the word "holiness" to mean the fullest possible love of God and the fullest possible love of others. The way of salvation includes the restoration of the image of Christ in the life of the believer. The great commandment of Christ summarizes the purpose of life. Life's goal is to love God fully and to love all freely.

The Wesleys hardly stood alone in this conviction. In emphasizing this lofty goal of holiness, they took their place in a lengthy succession of Christian disciples who became thoroughly captive to this biblical ideal. Some of the earliest followers of Jesus proclaimed that Christ became what we are so that we might become what he is. The ideal of Christlikeness—loving as Jesus loved—dawned early in the life of the church. A myriad of saints have embraced this vision through the ages. An anonymous slave sang with great resolve, "Lord, I want to be like Jesus, in my heart." The Wesleys simply held up this grand vision of a full, authentic Christlikeness before everyone's eyes. What made the Wesleyan vision unique was its refusal to separate holiness of heart (interior holiness) or love of God from holiness of life (exterior holiness) or love of neighbor. Nothing could be more important today.

The selections that follow focus attention on a Wesleyan practical theology of love. They explore the way of salvation—a dynamic, relational process that redeems and restores God's beloved children through the power of grace and love. The Wesleys celebrate the way in which our entire existence is enveloped by the wooing activity of God. They define the substance of their practical theology in the language of faith working by love leading to holiness of heart and life.

No sermon of John Wesley's articulates this central message of faith working by love better than "The Scripture Way of Salvation." Published in 1765, it reminds his readers that in the Christian life, everything revolves around grace. In his standard sermons, Wesley included thirteen discourses on Jesus's Sermon on the Mount (Matthew 5-7). In Sermon IV (1758) of that series he challenges the reader to a life of Christian wholeness as the fruit of faith. He characterizes Christianity as a social religion in which personal, saving faith is necessarily integrated with social, redemptive action. Genuine love works like this.

———◆———

SELECTIONS ON A PRACTICAL THEOLOGY OF LOVE

The Way of Salvation

Our main doctrines which include all the rest are three: repentance, faith, and holiness. The first of these we account, as it were, the porch of religion; the next, the door; the third, religion itself.

Works 9:227

Salvation begins with what is usually termed "prevenient grace," including the first wish to please God, the first dawn of light concerning God's will, and the first slight, transient conviction of having sinned against God. Salvation is carried on by "convincing grace," usually in scripture termed "repentance," which brings a larger measure of self-knowledge and a farther deliverance from the heart of stone. Afterwards we experience the proper Christian salvation whereby through grace we are saved by faith, consisting of those two grand branches, justification and sanctification. By justification we are saved from the guilt of sin and restored to the favor of God. By sanctification we are saved from the power and root of sin and restored to the image of God. The purpose of salvation is to have our hearts filled with pure love to God and neighbor. But even that love increases more and more until we grow in every way, measured by the standard of the fullness of Christ.

Works 3:203-204

**Reflect on or share your own narrative
of redemption. At what points does your
experience align with or depart from what
the Wesleys call "the way of salvation?"**

Enveloped in Grace

Allowing that all people's souls are dead in sin by nature, this excuses none, because no one is in a state of mere nature. No persons, unless they have quenched the Spirit, are wholly devoid of the grace of God. No one living is entirely destitute of natural conscience. But this is not natural, it is more properly termed prevenient grace. Everyone has some measure of God's light, some faint glimmering ray, which sooner or later, more or less, enlightens everyone that comes into the world. None of us sins because we are devoid of grace; rather, we sin because we do not embrace the grace that surrounds us.

Works, 3:207

Repent, that is, know yourselves. Awake, then, you who are sleeping. Acknowledge your brokenness and how it distorts what God intends you to be.

Works, 1:225-26

Come, all weary sinners, come,
    You who groan to bear your load,
Jesus calls his wanderers home;
    Hasten to your pardoning God.
Come, all guilty spirits oppressed,
    Answer to the Savior's call,
"Come, and I will give you rest,
    Come, and I will save you all."

Weary of this war within,
    Weary of this endless strife,
Weary of ourselves and sin,
    Weary of a wretched life;
Fain we would on you rely,
    Cast on you our sin and care,
To your arms of mercy fly,
    Find our lasting quiet there.

Burdened with a world of grief,
    Burdened with our sinful load,
Burdened with this unbelief,
    Burdened with the wrath of God,
Lo! We come to you for ease,
    True and gracious as you are,
Now our groaning soul release,
    Write forgiveness on our heart.

Redemption Hymns, 12-13

**Reflect upon or share a story about a
time you were weary or burdened and
God's grace carried you through.**

Faith

If drawn by your alluring grace,
    My lack of living faith I feel,
Show me in Christ your smiling face;
    What flesh and blood can ne'er reveal,
Your co-eternal Son display,
And call my darkness into day.

The gift unspeakable impart,
    Command the light of faith to shine,
To shine in my dark drooping heart,
    And fill me with the life divine;
Now bid the new creation be,
O God, let there be faith in me!

Redemption Hymns, 18-19

Justification is another word for pardon. It is the forgiveness of all our sins and (what is necessarily implied therein) our acceptance with God. The immediate effects of justification are the peace of God, a peace that exceeds all understanding and a joy unspeakable in the hope in God's glory.

Works 2:157-58

If any Christian doctrines may be properly termed fundamental they are doubtless these two—the doctrine of justification and that of the new birth. The former relates to that great work God does for us in forgiving our sins; the latter to the great work God does in us in renewing our fallen nature. Neither of these comes before the other. In the moment we are justified by the grace of God through the redemption that is in Jesus we are also born of the Spirit.

Works 2:187

Long my imprisoned spirit lay,

    Fast bound in sin and nature's night;

Thine eye diffused a quickening ray;

    I woke, the dungeon flamed with light;

My chains fell off, my heart was free,

I rose, went forth, and followed thee.

HSP (1739), 118

Show your faith in good works. Without these, all pretensions to faith are false. Good works are not the cause but the evidence of our new birth. The faith that does not work by love is an idle, barren, dead faith. It is no faith at all.

CW Sermons, 150-51

Let us plead for faith *alone*,

Faith which by our works is shown;

God it is who justifies,

Only faith the grace *applies*;

Active faith that lives within,
Conquers hell and death and sin,
Hallows whom it first made whole,
Forms the Savior in the soul.

Let us for this faith contend,
Sure salvation is its end;
Heaven already is begun,
Everlasting life is won.

Only let us persevere
Till we see our Lord appear,
Never from the Rock remove,
Saved by faith which works by love.

HSP (1740), 183-84

**The readings in this section relate to what
many of us would describe quite simply as
"conversion." Reflect on or tell your "conversion
story" and consider its importance in your life.**

Holiness

Sanctification begins the moment we are justified, in the holy,
humble, gentle, patient love of God. It gradually increases from that
moment, as a grain of mustard seed which at first is the least of seeds,
but afterwards puts forth large branches and becomes a great tree.
The heart is cleansed and filled with pure love to God and all people.

But even that love increases more and more until we are fully grown, measured by the standard of the fullness of Christ.

Works 3:204

God wills that I should holy be;
   That holiness I long to feel,
That full divine conformity
   To all my Savior's righteous will.
See, Lord, the travail of your soul
   Accomplished in the change of mine,
And plunge me, every part made whole,
   In all the depths of love divine.

Scripture Hymns, 2:324

Can a Christian be perfected in love in this life? What does it mean? It is complying with that kind command, "Give me your heart." It is loving the Lord your God with all your heart, and with all your soul, and with all your mind." This is the sum of Christian perfection. It is comprised in that one word, love. The first branch of it is the love of God, and as they that love God love their brothers and sisters also, it is inseparably connected with the second, "You will love your neighbor as yourself." You shall love everyone as your own soul, as Christ loved us. These contain the whole of Christian perfection.

Work 3:74-75

What is true religion then? It is easy to answer. It lies in one single point. It is neither more nor less than love. It is the love that fulfills the law—love that flows from a pure heart. True religion is the love of God and our neighbor; that is, every human being. This love, ruling the whole life, shaping all our attitudes and dispositions, directing all our thoughts, words, and actions, is pure and faultless religion.

Works 3:189

Jesu, thy boundless love to me
    No thought can reach, no tongue declare;
O knit my thankful heart to thee
    And reign without a rival there!
Thine wholly, thine alone, I am;
Be thou alone my constant flame!

O grant that nothing in my soul
    May dwell, but thy pure love alone!
O may thy love possess me whole,
    My joy, my treasure, and my crown;
Strange flames far from my heart remove—
My every act, word, thought, be love.

HSP (1739), 156-59

**Reflect upon or share your experience
of or relationship with a person who
seemed to be fully loving. What would
you like to do in your own life to be more
fully loving toward God and others.**

The Scripture Way of Salvation

You are saved by God's grace because of your faith.
This salvation is God's gift. It's not something
you possessed (Ephesians 2:8).

1. The true religion of Jesus Christ is plain and simple. The purpose of religion is, in one word, "salvation." The means to attain it is "faith." These two words express the essence of the gospel. But what does salvation mean, what kind of faith saves, and how does it save?

What is Salvation?

2. Salvation is not merely going to heaven or looking forward to eternal happiness. It is a present reality, a blessing which you may possess now through the free mercy of God. Salvation here refers to the entire work of God, from the first dawning of grace in the soul to its consummation in glory. The two main parts of salvation are "justification" and "sanctification."

3. Justification means pardon. God accepts us as we are and forgives all our sins. The death, resurrection, and righteousness of Christ reveal God's love to us and enable us to experience this pardon. The immediate effect of this pardon is the peace of God. We cannot fully understand it but it enables us to rejoice in the hope of the glory of God.

4. When God justifies us—when we experience pardon—in that very moment, the process of sanctification begins. In that instant we are born again, born from above, born of the Spirit. A real change in our hearts accompanies our change of relationship with God. We are

inwardly renewed by the power of God. From the time of our being born again, the gradual work of sanctification—becoming more and more like Christ—takes place. We die to sin and become increasingly alive to God.

5. St. Paul describes this process as "going on to perfection." But what is perfection? The word has various senses. Here it means perfect love. It is love excluding sin, love filling the heart, taking up the whole capacity of the soul. It is love always rejoicing, praying without ceasing, and in everything giving thanks.

**Describe your understanding of "salvation"
in a single sentence. What are the similarities
and differences between your view and those
of others with whom you journey in life?**

What is Saving Faith?

6. Scripture defines faith, in general, as a certainty in those things we cannot see. To have faith means to trust in God, to be sure of the things we hope for. You can think of it like a kind of spiritual light, sight, or perception. Through this gift we receive Christ in all his offices as our prophet, priest, and Lord.

7. In a more particular sense, faith gives us a certainty not only that God was in Christ reconciling the world to himself, but that Christ loves me and gave himself for me. Faith necessarily implies an assurance of these things. Given the nature of human experience, this assurance often precedes the certainty. For no one can have a childlike trust in God until he or she experiences adoption as a child of God. God saves us through this gift of faith.

**If faith means "trust," reflect on or talk about a
time in your life you really had to trust in God.**

How are We Saved by Faith into Love?

8. First, how is our relationship with God restored by faith? Trust is all we need to experience this restoration. Without trust in God, no one is justified. Nothing is right. But whenever anyone entrusts their life to God, that person is justified. People may repent, but they are not justified until they believe. The moment they do believe, with or without previous repentance, they are at one with God. Repentance and its fruits are only remotely necessary; but faith is immediately and directly necessary to justification.

9. Second, we are sanctified as well as justified by faith. In the same way we are made one with God by faith, so we are made holy by faith. No one can be holy without complete trust in God. But all who have experienced God's pardon and love must translate that experience into good works. For without them no one can grow in grace, in the image of Christ, or in the mind which was in Christ. In fact, without good works, God's children will fall out of sync with that new relationship they have with God based on grace.

10. Both repentance rightly understood and the practice of good works are necessary to growth in holiness of heart and life. But repentance following God's pardon is widely different from that which precedes it. Repentance after justification is a conviction of sin that remains in our hearts although it no longer reigns. It is a conviction of our continuing proneness to fall away from God even after we have been found by God. This also implies our continuing

helplessness apart from Christ. We must always remember that God's free grace comes before any of our inclinations to do what is good and then accompanies us every moment.

11. But what good works are necessary to holiness of heart and life? First, all works of piety such as public, family, and private prayer, receiving the Lord's Supper, searching the scriptures by hearing, reading, meditating, and fasting. Second, all works of mercy, whether they relate to people's physical or spiritual needs: feeding the hungry, clothing the naked, entertaining the stranger, visiting those in prison or are sick, endeavoring to instruct the uneducated; attempting to awaken sinners, to revive the lukewarm, to confirm those who waver, to comfort those who are discouraged, to be accountable for all in your care. This is how we grow in holiness in the direction of perfect love.

12. Because of this, you can sense the danger in the idea that there is no sin in a believer. Some Christians think that all sin is destroyed, root and branch, the moment a person is converted. But if you do not repent of the sin that remains in your life after conversion, the way to holiness is blocked. There is no need or room for growth in grace after conversion in such a view.

13. If you have any hope of continuing to grow in love, then you need to be vigilant in repenting of those remains of sin. This self-understanding is so important as a means toward the goal of loving God and neighbor as Christ has loved us. Even having said this, however, it is equally important to remember that perfect love—like every aspect of our salvation—is a gift. Only faith is immediately and directly necessary to sanctification.

14. What is that faith, then, by which we are sanctified and perfected in love? It is a certainty that God has promised a fully loving

heart each to us. Whatever God has promised, the Spirit is able to realize in the lives of God's children. God is willing and able to conform you to Christ and restore his image in you now.

> But if we live in the light in the same way as he is in the light, we have fellowship with each other, and the blood of Jesus, his Son, cleanses us from every sin (1 John 1:7).

15. When you think about the goal of holiness of heart and life, you can understand the inseparable connection between these three points:

Expect the fullness of love by faith.
Expect it as you are.
Expect it now.

To deny one of these is to deny them all. To allow one is to allow them all.

16. Do you believe we are made holy by our trust in God? Be true then to your principle and look for this blessing just as you are, neither better nor worse. As a poor sinner you still have nothing to pay, nothing to plead but Christ died for me. And if you look for it as you are, then expect it now. Christ is ready and he is all you want. He is waiting for you! He is at the door! Let your inmost soul cry out:

Come in, come in, thou heavenly Guest!
Nor hence again remove;
But sup with me and let the feast
Be everlasting love.

Works 2:153-69

**Wesley makes it clear that growth in
love is not a simple transaction. How do
you feel about this dynamic process by
which the Spirit fills us with love?**

Sermon on the Mount IV

You are the salt of the earth. But if salt loses its saltiness, how will
it become salty again? It's good for nothing except to be thrown
away and trampled under people's feet. You are the light of the
world. A city on top of a hill can't be hidden. Neither do people
light a lamp and put it under a basket. Instead, they put it on
top of a lampstand, and it shines on all who are in the house. In
the same way, let your light shine before people, so they can see
the good things you do and praise your Father who is in heaven
(Matthew 5:13-15).

1. In order to explain these important words I will show, first, that
Christianity is essentially a social religion, and that to turn it into a solitary religion is to destroy it; and second, that to conceal this religion
is impossible, as well as utterly contrary to its design. I shall, third,
answer some objections and conclude with a practical application.

Social Religion

2. By Christianity I mean that life of witness, service, and praise
revealed to us by Jesus Christ. When I say this is essentially a social
religion, I mean not only that it cannot exist very well, but that it

cannot exist at all apart from fellowship and witness with siblings in the family of God. It requires a loving and sharing community in mission. If Christians only practice their religion in isolation from others and the world, they destroy it.

3. I do not condemn solitude. All of us need time for personal and private reflection. Daily experience shows the absolutely necessity of quiet time with God. If you seek to be a real Christian, you need this. We all need to retreat daily from the world, at least morning and evening, to pray and to be nourished by intimate communion with God.

4. But solitude must not swallow up all our time. This would destroy and not advance true religion. All Christians need to cultivate the virtue of meekness. But to turn this into a solitary virtue destroys it. The same thing could be said of peace-making. How can a solitary Christian be an ambassador of reconciliation and mercy? How can a person isolated from other people grasp every opportunity of doing good to all people? The religion of Jesus Christ cannot exist without these social dimensions.

5. As a Christian, God has shaped you to season whatever is around you. God has designed us in such a way as to spread the divine savor on whatever we touch. The providence of God brings us into contact with so many other people for this very reason. Whatever grace we have received can be shared freely with others. You can influence others through your holy dispositions, words, and actions. You may never even know how wide that influence spreads.

6. Perhaps you were once excited about your life with God and eager to help others find happiness in life. But for whatever reason you lost your saltiness—if you have become flat, insipid, dead, both careless of your own soul and useless to the souls of others—how is

your saltiness to be restored? How shall you be recovered? What help is there? What hope? Can tasteless salt be restored to its savor?

What does "social religion" mean to you?

Bearing Witness to the Light

7. Some argue that salt conveys its savor without drawing any attention to itself. Isn't it better, they insist, to keep our religion to ourselves? Is it not simply something between us and God? No! As long as true religion—the religion of Jesus Christ—abides in our hearts, it is impossible to conceal it! To hide the light that God gives to us would be absolutely contrary to God's design.

8. Your love of God and neighbor makes you as conspicuous as the sun in the sky. You cannot escape life in this world. God has placed you here. In but not of the world, you bear witness to love to all humankind. You cannot flee from others. It is impossible for you to hide your lowliness and meekness and those other virtues by which you aspire to be perfect. Love cannot be hid any more than light; and least of all when it shines through your actions. Your patient and unwearied efforts to show love and mercy, to overcome evil with good, will make you still more visible and conspicuous than you were before.

9. If you are able to conceal your religion, it is not Christianity. Never even let the idea enter into your minds that you can hide your light.

10. What arguments could possibly be brought against this fundamental insight? Despite the persuasive power of scripture and

reason, however, some continue to make arguments for the superiority of a private or solitary religion. We need all the wisdom of God, therefore, to see through the snares. For many strong objections have been raised against a social, open, and active faith.

**Describe several ways by which you seek
to bear witness to the light in your life.**

Objections to Social Religion

11. First, it has been objected that religion does not lie in outward things. Rooted in the heart or inmost soul means that outward religion is worthless. Certainly, the root of religion lies in the heart, but if that root is truly alive, it will produce good fruit that is visible to everyone. Unquestionably, bare, outward religion in itself is worthless. But God delights in that genuine love and service produced by a pure and holy heart. God is pleased with the sacrifice of our prayers of praise and thanksgiving, with the sacrifice of our goods, when humbly devoted to God and used for the glory of Christ.

12. Second, some object that love is the only thing anybody needs. I grant that God only requires the love of God and neighbor springing from living faith. Without this, whatever we do or say really has no ultimate value. But it does not follow that love is an end in itself such that it supersedes either faith or good works. No! God has joined them together from the beginning of the world. No one should tear faith and love apart.

13. Since God is spirit, other object that we must worship God in spirit and in truth. Isn't this enough, they argue? Yes, it is, but

what does this mean? It means to believe in God as a wise, just, holy being, and yet merciful, gracious, and long-suffering. It means to love God, to delight in God, to desire God, with all our heart and mind and soul and strength. It means to imitate Christ by purifying ourselves, even as he is pure. It means to obey him whom we love, and in whom we believe, in thought and word and deed. Consequently, you cannot worship God correctly without keeping God's commandments. We must glorify God with our bodies as well as our spirits. We must practice good deeds with hearts lifted up to our Lord. We must make our daily work a sacrifice to God and offer our spiritual worship as the deepest expression of our gratitude to God.

14. The grand objection, however, is the appeal to experience. We focused our attention on outward works for many years, they argue, and it made no difference. I know that many have abused the means of grace, mistaking the means for the end of religion. Many suppose that attending church and receiving the sacraments, or simply trying to be good, either was the religion of Christ or would be accepted in its place. But let the abuse be taken away and the use remains. Engage in all those outward forms, therefore, in which God has promised to meet you. Practice them with a constant intention focused on the renewal of your soul in righteousness and true holiness—the deepening of your love for God and all others.

**Have you heard any of these objections
before and how do you feel about them?**

A Practical Application

15. Let your light shine—your lowliness of heart, your gentleness and meekness of wisdom; your serious, weighty concern for the things of God; your sorrow for the sins and miseries of all people; your earnest desire for universal holiness and full happiness in God; your tender goodwill to all your brother and sisters, and fervent love to God. Let it shine still more eminently in your actions, in your doing all possible good to all people and in all your efforts to establish peace with justice.

16. Only be careful not to seek your own praise. Avoid any desire to honor yourself. But let it be your sole aim that all who see your good works may glorify your loving God. Make this your one ultimate goal in all things. Be plain, open, and undisguised in living out this central purpose. Be honest and sincere in your dealings with all people that they may see the grace of God that resides within you. And although some will harden their hearts, others will perceive that you have been with Jesus.

17. Let the light that is in your heart shine in all good works, both acts of piety and acts of mercy. If you want to increase your ability to do good, renounce all luxuries. Cut off all unnecessary expenses, in food, in furniture, and in clothing. Be a good steward of every gift of God. In a word, be full of faith and love; do good; suffer evil. In your efforts to live by faith be steadfast and unmovable.

Works 1:531-49

**Reflect on or discuss several ways in which
you let your light of love shine in the world.**

3

How to Teach

Introduction to Wesleyan Spiritual Practices

The Spirit continues to renew the church today. We need to be reformed if we are going to speak and act with integrity concerning the needs of our world. But as United Methodists, renewal is part of our DNA. We began as a movement of renewal and we have always been open throughout our history to the revitalizing influence of God's Spirit. Just as in the life of an individual, so too in the life of the church, Christlikeness remains our ultimate goal.

Renewal often feels radical. Indeed, "radical" literally means to go to the source or origin of something, to rediscover the "root" (*radix*). So refreshing the church always sparks a new passion among Christ's followers to get back to basics, to unearth the roots, the treasures of our faith. In this time of uncertainty with regard to the future, we know we need to look back in order to move forward.

We need to rediscover who we are as United Methodists in the Wesleyan tradition.

Many of those things being rediscovered today are classic elements of renewal. It is exciting to realize that we are not alone in this journey. The path is actually well-trod. As we think about a future filled with hope, see if some of these elements don't ring true for you and your community of faith.

- Emphases on the experiential side of faith and the importance of a personal relationship with God in Christ
- Rediscovery of the Bible as the "living Word" and as the book of the people
- Elevation of the ministry of the laity as an essential expression of the priesthood of all believers
- Stress on mutual accountability and the strength drawn from intimate community, especially small groups
- Celebration of classic spiritual practices as important means of grace both in conversion and spiritual growth
- Renewed interest in the sacramental life of the church and liturgy as the work of the people
- Recovery of mission as the reason for the church's being and the importance of our partnership with God in God's mission of love in the world

In all this—the dynamic balance of life and Spirit, Spirit and Word, Word and sacrament, sacrament and life, life and mission—the internal and the external become vital means to a rediscovery of living and active faith.

The practices related to renewal constitute a curriculum in spiritual formation. The challenges of our time, both inside and outside the church, are complex. We seem to be tossed about, as the old hymn says. We have conflict inside the church and doubt about the future. Fighting within and fears about what is outside lead to blurred vision. We know that we cannot meet the challenges of our time without strong inner resources. Activities and programs cannot substitute for well-formed spiritual people. But spiritual formation was the heartbeat of the Wesleyan movement of renewal.

Moreover, the way in which we teach our faith must unite our concern for both individuals and society with a holistic understanding of people as thinking, feeling, and acting beings. To transmit the faith from one generation to the next means helping people understand, experience, and act upon the good news of Jesus Christ. In many ways this defines the mission of the church. Spiritual formation, therefore, prepares the committed disciple of Jesus to live God's way of love in the world.

I have been a theological educator my whole professional life. That means a lot of teaching. When many of us hear that word "teaching," we think of the classroom. I have learned over the years, however, that most people learn best by doing. So when we ask the question about how to teach, we need to shift our thinking from passive recipients to active participants. The Wesleys knew this. Moreover they were great teachers. Early Methodists learned the faith, not by studying it, but by doing it. They learned about God by immersing themselves in spiritual practices.

Means of Grace

Practices teach us how to open up spaces in our lives where the presence and power of God can be known and experienced. As in all previous periods of renewal, the church today has rediscovered the power of Eucharist. Since the second century and possibly in the New Testament itself, this term has referred to the sacrament of Holy Communion. Literally meaning "thanksgiving," the Eucharist has always been a vital, even a central, force in the formation of Christ's disciples. In the sacrament, we realize the unity of the individual and the community, reflection and action, cross and resurrection, remembrance and thanksgiving.

The power of the sacrament partially rests in the capacity of sign-acts to communicate the fullness of God's love and grace to the whole person. Words and signs, senses and action all combine through the power of the Holy Spirit to make the Eucharist a genuine place of divine encounter. It is the "visible Word" that confronts and comforts us in those areas of life the "spoken Word" cannot reach.

The words of a youth, written in a letter to her former pastor, reveal the transforming and forming power of this means of grace.

> When I received the bread and wine, I felt that I had found Christ, really found him, for the first time in my life. I can honestly say that receiving Holy Communion has become the most important part of the worship service to me. It teaches me who I am as a follower of Jesus. Participating in the sacrament helps me understand my faith.

Like this young disciple, many people today are pointing to the Eucharist as that place where God reminds us about who and whose we are, feeds us for our journey, and unites us in service to the world.

John and Charles Wesley's concern about spiritual renewal prompted their question about how to teach. How does the church offer Christ—offer God's grace—to a world in need of re-creation? Where do we learn about and encounter God? How can we find, or rather, how can we be found by God? How do we teach others the wonders of God's love which we have experienced in life? How do we teach the faith both to those within our communities and to those who eagerly await a good word in a broken world?

The Wesleys' simple answer to these questions was that all of us encounter and learn about God in those places Christ promised to be present. We call these places "means of grace." It is through these means that God transforms our lives, forms our spirits, and informs our actions. All this implies deep education. We encounter the living Word as the Spirit breathes new life into the words of scripture; when two or three are gathered in his name, Christ is in their midst; God meets us at the table and at our places of prayer to commune with us and empower us to serve.

In general, for the Wesleys there are several chief means of grace or "works of piety." Through the practices of 1) praying and fasting, 2) engaging scripture, 3) conferencing with other Christians (what we would call fellowship today), and 4) participating in the Lord's Supper, God gives and preserves a life of faith and holiness. We also encounter and experience God's grace through "works of mercy," including acts of compassion and acts of justice (which we will explore more fully in chapter 4). As you read through the selections on these places of divine/human encounter below, consider how your life has been changed and enriched by them. What have you learned through them? Have these been places where you have discovered the living Lord?

Faith Seeking Understanding in Practices

The practices in which the early Methodists engaged taught them about their faith and how to integrate faith into life. Practices enabled them to go more deeply into their faith. The progression they experienced was a movement from faith to fuller understanding. As authentic followers of Jesus they wanted to go deep, broad, high, and wide. Practices helped them discover the wonders of God's love.

The revival of the Wesleys, for example, was both evangelical and sacramental. Methodist people experienced the dynamic interrelation of Word and Table. Sacramental grace (embraced in Communion) and evangelical experience (a direct connection with the love of God in Christ) were viewed as necessary counterparts of a balanced Christian life. Together they helped them discover more fully who they were and what they were called to do. It is not too much to say that the unity of rich personal faith and abundant relational grace was the vital center of the Wesleyan message.

The means of grace were so important to John Wesley that he published a sermon of that title early in the life of the movement in 1746. It discusses the centrality of prayer, fellowship, and Holy Communion in particular. The previous year he and Charles had already published a collection of hymns on the Lord's Supper—166 hymns teaching their follower that the sacrament was a memorial of Christ's death, a sign and means of present grace, and a pledge of the heavenly banquet to come.

Toward the end of his life, in 1781, John Wesley published a sermon "On Zeal." The primary purpose of this sermon was to distinguish between true zeal—an expression of deep love for God and others—from religious zeal that often fans the flames of controversy and division. It has functioned primarily, however, as a guide to authentic Christian discipleship in the world.

Christian discipleship, if it bears the mark of the Wesleyan spirit, must be rooted in the means of grace. Spiritual formation true to this same spirit, moreover, will be eucharistic. Through these means God communicates the love revealed to us in Christ. Through the means of grace we learn of him and grow into his likeness.

SELECTIONS ON LEARNING BY DOING

Means of Grace

By "means of grace" I understand outward signs, words, or actions ordained by God and appointed for this purpose—to be the ordinary channels whereby God might convey preventing, justifying, or sanctifying grace to God's beloved children. The chief of these means are prayer, whether in private or in community; searching the Scriptures (which implies reading, hearing, and meditating on them) and receiving the Lord's Supper, eating bread and drinking wine in remembrance of Christ.

Works 1:381

One general avenue to enthusiasm, or religious fanaticism, is expecting the end without the means—expecting knowledge, for instance, without searching the scriptures and consulting the children of God; expecting spiritual strength without constant prayer and steady watchfulness; expecting any blessing without hearing the word of God at every opportunity.

Christian Perfection, 134

**Which "means of grace" do you
practice most regularly, and how has
this practice shaped your life?**

Prayer

O begin! Fix some part of every day for prayer. Whether you like it or not, read and pray daily. It is for your life. There is no other way. Otherwise you will be a trifler all your days.

Works 27:204

Perhaps no sin of omission more frequently occasions dullness of spirit than the neglect of private prayer. Nothing can replace a life of prayer. One thing is absolutely clear. The life of God in the soul does not continue, much less increase, unless we use all opportunities of communing with God and pouring out our hearts before God. If we neglect this, if we permit our work, our play, or any other distractions to take precedence over this spiritual practice, our life will surely decay.

Works 2:209

Pray, without ceasing pray,
   (Your Captain gives the word)
His summons cheerfully obey,
   And call upon the Lord;
   To God your every want
   In instant prayer display,

Pray always; pray, and never faint,

    Pray, without ceasing pray.

HSP (1749) 1:238

Prayer is the lifting up of the heart to God. All words of prayer without this are mere hypocrisy. Whenever therefore you attempt to pray, see that it is your one design to commune with God, to lift up your heart to God, to pour out your soul before God.

Works 1:575

**Reflect for a few moments on your own
life of prayer. What are some of the
ways in which you feel called to enhance
your life with God in prayer?**

Scripture

I showed concerning the Holy Scriptures, 1) that to search (i.e., read and hear them) is a command of God; 2) that this command is given to all, believers and unbelievers; 3) that this is commanded or ordained as a means of grace, a means of conveying the grace of God to all, whether unbelievers or believers, who by experience know that all scripture is useful in God's work of spiritual renewal.

Works 19:158

While in thy word we search for thee,

    (We search with trembling awe)

Open our eyes and let us see
   The wonders of thy law.

Now let our darkness comprehend
   The light that shines so clear;
Now the revealing Spirit send,
   And give us ears to hear.

HSP (1740), 41

In order to benefit the most from your reading of scripture: 1) Set apart a little time, if you can, every morning and evening for that purpose. 2) Read a chapter out of the Old and one out of the New Testament. If you cannot do this, take a single chapter or a part of one. 3) Read with singular focus to know the whole will of God and a fixed resolution to do it. 4) Give constant attention to the analogy of faith—the connection and harmony you discern with those grand, fundamental doctrines: repentance, faith, and inward and outward holiness 5) Pray seriously and earnestly whenever you engage scripture. Conclude your reading with prayer so that what you read may be written on your heart. 6) As you read, pause and examine yourself with regard to your heart and life. Put into immediate use whatever you have learned. Let there be no delay. Whatever you resolve, begin to execute the first moment you can. You will then find this word to be the power of God unto present and eternal salvation.

Works (Jackson), 14:253

**Which of Wesley's instructions about
engaging scripture touches you most deeply?
Why do you think this is the case?**

Fellowship

"Holy solitaries" is a phrase no more consistent with the gospel than holy adulterers. The gospel of Christ knows of no religion, but social; no holiness but social holiness.

Works (Jackson), 14:321

Help us to help each other, Lord,
　　Each other's cross to bear;
Let all their friendly aid afford,
　　And feel each other's care.

Help us to build each other up,
　　Our meager gifts improve,
Increase our faith, confirm our hope,
　　And perfect us in love.

HSP (1742), 83

As Methodists we watch over one another in love. We mark our growth in grace. We advise and exhort one another from time to time. We pray for one another and our needs. This, and this alone, is Christian fellowship. But where else is it to be found today? Look east or west, north or south. Name what church you please. Is this Christian fellowship there? Rather, are not the bulk of the parishioners a mere rope of sand? What Christian connection is there between them? What conversation about spiritual things? What watching over each other's souls? What bearing of one another's burdens? We introduce Christian fellowship where it was utterly destroyed. And the fruits of it have been peace, joy, love, and zeal for every good word and work.

Works 9:259

**Reflect upon or discuss a situation in which the
way someone "watched over you in love" made
a major difference in your life at that time.**

Eucharist

Fasting he doth and hearing bless,
    And prayer can much avail,
Good vessels all to draw the grace
    Out of salvation's well.

But none like this mysterious rite
    Which dying mercy gave
Can draw forth all God's promised might
    And all God's will to save.

This is the richest legacy
    Thou hast on us bestowed,
Here chiefly, Lord, we feed on thee,
    And drink thy precious blood.

HLS, 31

I showed at large, 1) that the Lord's Supper was ordained by
God to be a means of conveying to all either preventing or justifying
or sanctifying grace according to their several necessities; 2) that the
persons for whom it was ordained are all those who know and feel
that they want the grace of God, either to restrain them from sin or
to show their sins forgiven or to renew their souls in the image of

God; 3) that inasmuch as we come to Christ's table, not to give him anything, but to receive whatsoever he sees best for us, there is no previous preparation indispensably necessary but a desire to receive whatsoever he pleases to give; and 4) that no fitness is required at the time of communicating but a sense of our condition, of our utter helplessness.

Works, 19:159

Sure pledge of ecstasies unknown
    Shall this divine communion be,
The ray shall rise into a sun,
    The drop shall swell into a sea.

HLS, 87

Jesu, we thus obey
    your last and kindest word,
Here in your own appointed way
    We come to meet our Lord;
    The way you have enjoined
    You will therein appear:
We come with confidence to find
    Your special presence here.

    Our hearts we open wide
    To make the Savior room:
And lo! the Lamb, the crucified,
    The sinner's friend, is come!
    His presence makes the feast,

And now our bosoms feel
The glory not to be expressed,
The joy unspeakable.

HLS, 69

**Reflect upon or discuss one of your favorite
memories at the Lord's Table. How does
that experience, and others at the table,
continue to shape who you are?**

The Means of Grace

Ever since the time of your ancestors,
you have deviated from my laws
and have not kept them (Malachi 3:7).

1. Are there any means ordained by God as the usual channels of saving grace? This question could never have been proposed in the early church. The whole body of Christians believed Christ taught his disciples about practices that lavish grace upon God's children. Their constant practice set this beyond all dispute. "The believers devoted themselves to the apostles' teaching, to the community, to their shared meals, and to their prayers" (Acts 2:42).

2. In the following sermon, I propose to examine whether there are any means of grace. By means of grace I mean outward signs, words, or actions established by God and appointed to be the ordinary channels by which God conveys grace to persons in search of life.

Primary Channels of Grace

3. The primary channels of grace are prayer, whether in private or within the context of worship; searching the scriptures (which implies reading, hearing, and meditating upon them); and receiving the Lord's Supper, eating bread and drinking wine in remembrance of Christ. These we believe to be ordained by God as the ordinary means by which God relates to us and offer the grace of Christ through the power of the Holy Spirit.

4. The whole value of these means depends on their actual subservience to the purpose of religion. All these means, if separated from their end, are less than nothing and empty actions. If they do not lead to the knowledge and love of God, they do not good to anyone. Whoever imagines there is any intrinsic power in the means themselves does not properly understand them. For we know that there is no inherent value in the words that are spoken in prayer, in the letter of scripture read, or the bread and wine received in the Lord's Supper.

5. God alone is the giver of every gift. It is only owing to God that there is any blessing conveyed to our souls through any of these means. Indeed, the great foundation of the whole Christian building is salvation by grace through faith. You are saved from your sins and restored to the favor and image of God, not by any of your own works but by the free grace, the mere mercy of God through the merits of God's well-beloved Son.

6. But the main question remains. If salvation is the gift and the work of God, how do we attain it? Our Lord has shown us the way in the Word! According to holy scripture, all who desire the grace of God are to wait for it in the means of grace that God has ordained in using them rather than neglecting them.

Have you developed a regular pattern of
immersing yourself in these means of grace?
What words of wisdom do you have to share with
others about this pattern for spiritual formation?

Prayer

7. First, all who desire the grace of God are to wait for it in the way of prayer. This is the express instruction of our Lord himself. In his Sermon on the Mount he says: "Ask, and you will receive. Search, and you will find. Knock, and the door will be opened to you" (Matthew 7:7). How could our blessed Lord more plainly declare that we may enrich our relationship with God by this means.

Searching the Scriptures

8. Second, we are to wait for God's grace in searching the scriptures. Our Lord's direction with regard to the use of this means is equally plain and clear. "Examine the scriptures," he says. "They also testify about me" (John 5:39). He instructed them to study the Word in order that they might believe in him.

9. God richly blesses those who read and meditate on the Word. Through this means God not only gives, but also confirms and increases true wisdom. Paul admonishes Timothy: "Since childhood you have known the holy scriptures that help you to be wise in a way that leads to salvation through faith that is in Christ Jesus" (2 Timothy 3:15). He was far from making light of the Hebrew scriptures then. He found power and light in the wholeness of scripture. If you

read, study, and value the totality of God's Word, you will not wander or go wrong. Let all, therefore, who desire that day of salvation to dawn upon their hearts, wait for it in searching the scriptures.

The Lord's Supper

10. Third, all who desire an increase in the grace of God are to wait for it in partaking of the Lord's Supper. In this too, Jesus' direction is clear: "I received a tradition from the Lord, which I also handed on to you: on the night on which he was betrayed, the Lord Jesus took bread. After giving thanks, he broke it and said, 'This is my body, which is for you; do this to remember me'" (1 Corinthians 11:23-24). The command first given by our Lord is expressly repeated by the apostle: "Eat from the bread and drink from the cup" (1 Corinthians 11:28). These words not only imply permission, but a clear and explicit command.

11. Eating of that bread and drinking of that cup is the outward and visible means by which God conveys that inward and spiritual grace to our lives. God offers to us that righteousness and peace and joy in the Holy Spirit that was promised through the body of Christ once given and the blood of Christ once shed for us. Let all, therefore, who truly desire the grace of God eat the bread and drink the cup!

**How are prayer, scripture, and Holy
Communion interconnected in a holistic
vision of spiritual formation? What part of
your life does each of these means touch?**

Objections Answered

12. Some people have raised objections against the use of these means of grace. They first and chief of these is that you cannot practice these means without trusting in them. But what do you mean by trusting in them? Believing that if you wait in this way you shall attain what otherwise you would not? By the grace of God I will thus trust in them till the day I die. I will believe that whatever God has promised, God will be faithful to perform. And seeing God has promised to bless me in this way, I trust it shall be according to the Word.

13. Second, some say that this is seeking salvation through works. But what is seeking salvation by works? In the writings of Paul it means either seeking to be saved by observing the ritual works of the Old Testament law or by expecting salvation for the sake of our own works, by the merit of our own righteousness. But how is either of these implied in my waiting in the way God has ordained, by expecting to meet God where God has promised to be?

14. Third, some vehemently object that Christ is the only means of grace. When you say that Christ is the means of grace, you mean that he is the sole price and purchaser of it. But who denies this! Seeing that grace is the gift of God, we are undoubtedly to wait on God for salvation. But if God has appointed the way for us to wait, can you devise a better plan? That great truth must stand unshaken: all who desire the grace of God are to wait for it in the means that God has ordained.

**Which of Wesley's answers to these objections
is most compelling to you and why?**

Directions on Using the Means of Grace

15. It is important to know how to use the means of grace properly with regard, first, to their order. There is a kind of natural order by which God usually employs these means in bringing a seeker to redemption. God often encounters people or confronts them when they least expect it. Someone may be awakened by a sermon or conversation, by a tragedy, or by an immediate conviction through the Spirit. The seeker purposely goes to hear how he or she may be saved. Hearing and reading the scriptures leads to more intentional meditation.

16. Such persons begin to talk about the things of God and to pray. They want to pray with those who know God. In worship they notice others who go to the Table of the Lord. They consider that Christ said to do this. After struggling with their scruples about being too great a sinner, or being unfit or not worthy, they break through. They continue in God's way—hearing, reading, meditating, praying and partaking of the Lord's Supper—until God speaks to their heart through the power of the Spriit: "Your faith has saved you. Go in peace" (Luke 7:50).

17. Our understanding of this natural progression can help us in leading persons step by step through the means. An understanding of the stages of faith should inform our discussion in these spiritual matters and guide us in our recommendations. Yet as we find no command in scripture for any particular order to be observed, so neither do the providence and the Spirit of God adhere to any without variation. The means into which different people are led and in which they find the blessing of God, are varied, transposed, and combined a thousand different ways.

18. The sure and general rule for all who groan for redemption is this: Whenever opportunity serves, use all the means that God has ordained. For who knows in which God will meet you with the grace that brings salvation?

19. With regard to the proper manner of practicing the means of grace, first, it is important to remember that God is always above all means. Do not limit the Almighty. God can convey the grace of Christ either in or outside any of the means that have been appointed. Look then every moment for God's appearing! God is always ready; always willing; always able to save.

20. Second, before you use any means, consider carefully that there is no power in this alone. The means are in themselves poor, dead, empty things. Separate from God every means is a dry leaf, a shadow. Neither is there any merit in your practicing them; nothing intrinsically pleasing to God. But because God bids, therefore I do. Because God directs me to wait in this way, therefore I wait here for God's free mercy and love.

21. Third, in using all the means, seek God alone. In and through every outward work focus your attention on the power of God's Spirit and the merits of God's Son. Nothing short of God can satisfy your soul. Therefore, keep your eye on God in all, through all, and above all. Use all the means as means; as ordained, not for their own sake, but in order to renew your soul in righteousness and true holiness.

22. After you have practiced any of these means, be careful about how you value yourself, how you congratulate yourself for having done some great thing. This is turning all into poison. If God was there, if God's love flowed into your heart, you have forgotten, as

it were, the outward work. You see, you know, you feel that God is all in all. Give God all the praise! Glorify God in all things through Jesus Christ!

Works 1:376-97

**Which of these practical directions do you feel
you need to implement in your own life and why?**

EXTRACTS FROM ON ZEAL

It is good to be zealously affected always in a good thing (KJV).

1. Zeal is one of the most important aspects of religion. Zeal is essential to love of God and neighbor. On the other hand, nothing is more dangerous. Persecution and zeal are closely related.

2. It is possible to distinguish right from destructive zeal, but this is often a very difficult task.

3. We must distinguish true Christian zeal, therefore, from its various counterfeits. This is all the more important because there seems to be so much more religious zeal today.

4. For good or ill, right and wrong zeal are very much part of our world today. Let us see if we cannot separate these, that we may avoid the latter, and affirm the former. Three questions are critical to our task: 1) What is the nature of true Christian zeal? and 2) What are its characteristics?

True Christian Zeal

5. The word "zeal" means heat. When it is figuratively applied to the mind, it means any warm emotion or affection. Frequently we associate it with anger and indignation; sometimes with vehement desire. Religious zeal refers to situations in which our passions are strongly moved on a religious account, whether for or against something.

6. This kind of zeal is not properly religious or Christian zeal if it be not loving. True zeal must be oriented toward the love of God and our neighbor. Many people do not understand that Christian zeal is all love. It is nothing else. The love of God and neighbor fills up its whole nature.

7. True Christian zeal is fervent love. It is nothing other than the flame of love. This is the nature, the inmost essence, of good or right zeal.

**Our world seems to be full of a lot of
zeal today. What forms of zeal have you
witnessed and reflect upon or discuss which
are good and which are bad in your view.**

Characteristics of Christian Zeal

8. The properties of love, therefore, are the properties of zeal also. One of the chief properties of love is humility. However great one's zeal might be, it must be matched with the same level of humility; they must rise and fall together. If you are filled with zeal for God, that means that you view yourself as little, and poor, and vile in your own eyes.

9. Love is meek. True zeal, then, teaches us to be meek, as well as lowly; to be equally superior to anger or pride. Wax melts in a fire. In the same way, before the sacred flame of zeal, all turbulent passions melt away, and leave the soul unruffled and serene.

10. Love is characterized by unwearied patience. True zeal, then, enables us to be content in all circumstances. Rather than complaining or murmuring, we give thanks in everything because of our zeal for the Lord.

11. A fourth property of Christian zeal deserves greater consideration. Paul writes that "it's always good to have people concerned about you with good intentions, and not just when I'm there with you" (Galatians 4:18). He implies that zeal ought not to be a transient disposition, but that it ought to be steady and deeply rooted. If something is good, we ought to be constantly zealous about it.

12. But what is good in the sight of God? What is that form of religion in which God is always well pleased? In a Christian believer love sits upon the throne which is erected in the inmost soul. Love of God and neighbor fills the whole heart and reigns without a rival there. In a circle near the throne are all the holy dispositions—long-suffering, gentleness, meekness, fidelity, temperance—everything comprising the mind which was in Christ Jesus. In an exterior circle are all the works of mercy, whether to the souls or bodies of men. By these we exercise our Christlike dispositions, improving them, so that all these works are real means of grace. Next to these are those practices usually described as works of piety: reading and hearing the Word; public, family, private prayer; receiving the Lord's supper; fasting or abstinence. Lastly, that Christ's followers may more effectually provoke each other to love and and good works, our blessed Lord has united them together in the church.

13. This is that religion that our Lord has established. This is the entire, connected system of Christianity. From the lowest point to the highest, love is enthroned in the heart.

14. Every Christian, therefore, ought to be zealous for the church, affectionately connected with it and earnestly desiring its prosperity. All of us ought to be zealous about the church universal, praying for it continually, and particularly concerned about our own community of faith.

15. We ought to be even more zealous for the means of grace, ordained by Christ, than for the church itself. Our zeal ought to burn for prayer, for the Lord's supper, for immersing ourselves in scripture, and for the much-neglected duty of fasting. We should earnestly recommend these by example and then by exhortation, as often as we can.

16. We should demonstrate our zeal for works of piety, but much more for works of mercy. If our practice of piety interferes with opportunities to practice justice and compassion, we should defer to the latter. We should even omit our study of scripture and prayer, or postpone them, if loving service calls for our immediate action.

17. But as zealous as we are for all good works, we should still be more zealous for growth in Christlike character. We must study to be humble, meek. gentle, long-suffering, contented, resigned to the will of God, dead to the world and truly alive to God. For these proofs and fruits of living faith we cannot be too zealous. We should make them the continual matter of our life of prayer; as being far more important than any outward works.

18. Our choicest zeal should be reserved for love itself, for love fulfills all that God commands. The church, the sacraments, works of piety and mercy, all other holy dispositions, are inferior to love.

They rise in value only as they approach nearer and nearer to love. Here then is the great object of Christian zeal. Pray fervently for your hearts to be more and more enlarged in love to God and to all humanity. Do this one thing. Press on for the prize of God's upward call in Christ Jesus.

Works 3:308-21

What do you think you can do to make sure your zeal remains healthy and Christian—loving?

4

What to Do

Introduction to Wesleyan Missional Practice

People sometimes conceive Christlikeness as an exclusively interior aspect of spirituality. This is not biblical. Neither is it consistent with the way in which God has made us. God created us holistically, so our spirituality must be holistic as well. We are not only thinking and feeling creatures; we are action-oriented as well. We can even see our three-part composition in the questions John Wesley posed at that inaugural Methodist Conference. What to teach aligns with the intellectual part of our lives. Our experiential aspect relates to how we teach and learn. As people made for action, we must always be asking, What are we called to do?

Neither is Christlikeness something exclusively individualistic. Communities can be like Christ as well. God calls the community of faith to reflect the values and the qualities we see in Jesus. Unfortunately, many people who consider themselves to be faithful

Christians don't seem to resemble Jesus. That is particularly problematic and compromises our witness in the world to the truth about love. Moreover, many Christians exhibit values and qualities diametrically opposed to the way of Jesus. The same can be said of the church. This kind of hypocrisy characterized church life in the time of the Wesleys as well. Little wonder that people, then and now, are not drawn to the church when something other than love dominates the motives and actions of people who claim to follow Jesus. But whenever people feel valued and loved, they respond enthusiastically.

John and Charles Wesley's rediscovery of the church as God's mission of love fueled their movement of renewal. They believed that God designed the church as a redemptive community, a family that lives in and for God's vision of shalom in the world. The church draws committed Christian disciples perennially to Jesus and to one another in community (centripetal movement) and then spins them out into the world in mission and service (centrifugal movement). The Wesleys' missional practice mirrored their understanding of God—the loving Creator who was active and at work in the world to save and restore all creation. In this vision they refused to separate faith and works, personal salvation and social justice, physical and spiritual needs.

Works of Mercy

In early Methodism, those who encountered the good news of the gospel and were drawn into communities of love were propelled into the world with a mission of witness and service. The Wesleys excluded no one from this imperative to share the love they had received and experienced for themselves. The Wesleyan way, therefore, includes an essential concern for active social service, commitment to the poor, and advocacy for the spiritually, politically, and socially oppressed. They considered all this to be a critical aspect of their love of neighbor—a mission of compassion and justice.

The early Methodists found it impossible to separate their personal experience of God and devotion to Christ from their active role as agents of reconciliation and social transformation in the world. The primary means by which they lived out this holistic understanding of the Christian life was through "works of mercy." These practices paralleled the more interior works of piety. John Wesley mandated that his followers practice mercy which he defined in the second of his "General Rules" in the most expansive way possible—"do good." They shared God's love freely with others by befriending the poor, feeding the hungry, empowering the destitute, and comforting the neglected. They visited prisons, established orphanages and schools, and practiced this servant-oriented faith by loving others freely. These activities extended the ministry of Methodism into the communities they served. They shared God's love with everyone.

The Restoration of Justice

Amos saw the vital connection between love of God and the struggle for justice. Our world is divided between haves and have nots. Abject poverty for many is the price of affluence for the few. No society will ever last if it is built on the foundations of oppression and injustice. Mary, in her Song of Praise, proclaims that God fills the hungry with good things, but sends the rich away empty. God lifts up the lowly and topples the mighty from their seats of power. God's new age is characterized by a radical reversal of place; it is an upside-down kingdom.

In his struggle for justice in racially-torn South Africa, Desmond Tutu boldly proclaimed that the Christian is either in favor of evil or in favor of good, either on the side of the oppressed or on the side of the oppressor. No true disciple of Jesus can be neutral. Being a Christian today means being engaged in the struggle for justice. It means embracing the Christlike role of anti-racism in an age of resurgent racism and xenophobia. This struggle is ultimately a quest to free all of God's children, oppressed and oppressor alike. To become Christlike means to partner with God in the work of establishing justice in an unjust world.

Embracing Nonviolence and Peace

Not only is our world unjust, it is violent. In the United States, gun violence continues to plague our communities and destroy the lives of families and communities. We are all affected by that violence in one way or another. Self-esteem is destroyed in many of our children—a violation of our hope for the future. Domestic abuse remains rampant—a violation of the right of women, in particular, to live in safety and peace. The threat of mass destruction because of our modern weapons holds us all hostage—a violation of our freedom to live faithfully in the present. Our choice today, as Dr. Martin Luther King Jr. prophesied more than half a century ago, is not between violence and nonviolence, but between nonviolence and nonexistence. What can we do?

Christ announced and embodied the inbreaking of a new rule in life. Through the prophet Isaiah, God proclaimed a glorious vision of the way life is meant to be: "Then they will beat their swords into iron plows and their spears into pruning tools. Nation will not take up sword against nation; they will no longer learn how to make war"

(Isaiah 2:4). Isaiah asserts that authentic love and integrity create peace; only justice can produce lasting security.

The psalmist echoes the theme: "Faithful love and truth have met; righteousness and peace have kissed" (Psalm 85:10). To be a disciple of the Prince of Peace means daring to hope in the struggle for justice that brings peace. In performing God's Word—in embodying the vision—we become a presence of healing and reconciliation in our violent world. To do God's will is to model our ministry upon our Lord's example of solidarity with the poor, liberation of the oppressed, and nonviolence in the face of evil.

The Wesleyan Witness

When you turn to the selections from the Wesleys' in this chapter, you will be struck by the contemporary ring of their words. You might even ask, Has anything really changed from that time to our own? While the shape of human problems changes, the issues remain perennial. Innocent people suffer. The abuse of power and the corrupting influence of greed lead to various forms of human bondage. Violent conflict shatters lives. In the midst of these circumstances, Methodist people throughout our history valiantly offered Christ in word and deed, witness and service. They loved God deeply. But they also loved God's world by partnering with God in God's mission of love. They lived in and for God's vision of shalom.

They loved their neighbor by engaging in God's good work of doing justice, waging peace, and building loving communities in which every person has a place. John Wesley believed that the decline in genuine Christianity in his own time was due to the failure of Christians to identify with the poor—the least, last, and lost. Have we lost those connections in our own time? Solidarity with the poor and marginalized required that he confront the unjust structures of his own society and church. Not only did he expose injustice wherever he found it, he waged peace as one of the noblest forms of Christian love.

All three of the treatises presented here were written by Wesley during the critical decade of the 1770s. They reflect the maturity and wisdom of a man who had confronted tremendous evil and emerged with his optimism in God's grace and the power of love unshaken.

In his *Thoughts on the Present Scarcity of Provisions* (1773), he attempts to address the issue of hunger in its larger context as a major social evil linked with poverty. Not satisfied with the response of many simply to relieve the symptoms, his concern is to identify the root causes of hunger. His discussion of the problem reveals his consistent understanding of the interconnectedness of life.

Wesley wrote his *Thoughts on Slavery* in the early months of 1774. The port city of Bristol, one of Methodism's primary bases of operation in the early years of the movement, was heavily dependent on the slave trade. He knew the dangers of speaking out against this unjust and inhumane system. But he refused to abdicate his calling as an advocate for the oppressed. The phrase "justice, mercy, and truth" echoes throughout the treatise.

When he wrote his *Seasonable Address by a Lover of Peace* in 1776 (note the date), England was locked in a bitter conflict with the American colonies. His primary concern was to do all he could to bring an end to that fratricidal war. In fact, the American Revolution evoked some of his strongest anti-war rhetoric. He provides a model of nonviolent conflict resolution that stands in direct opposition to standard models of military intervention. In his view, he was simply seeking to be Christlike in his response to life in a broken world.

Christlikeness entails loving the unlovable and the enemy. To be a follower of Jesus means partnering with God in God's mission of love in the world.

◆

SELECTIONS ON LOVING WITNESS AND SERVICE

The Work of Love

To serve the present age,
My calling to fulfil;
O may it all my powers engage
To do my Master's will!

Scripture Hymns, 1:58

Do good! Do all the good you can. Let your plenty supply your neighbor's needs. There is always something you can do. If you really considered our Lord's command, you would never ask, "What shall I do?"

Works 4:133-34

Let love not visit you as a transient guest, but be the constant ruling disposition of your soul. See that your heart is filled at all times and on all occasions with real, genuine love, not to those only that love you, but to every soul. Let it pant in your heart, let it sparkle in your eyes, let it shine on all your actions. Whenever you open your lips, let it be with love, and let the law of kindness be on your tongue. Your word will then distill as the rain and as the dew upon the tender herb. Be not constrained or limited in your affection, but let it embrace every child of God. Everyone that is born of a woman has a claim to your goodwill. You owe this not to some, but to all. And let all people know that you desire both their temporal and eternal happiness as sincerely as you do your own.

Works 3:422-23

If so low a child as I
 May to thy great glory live,
All my actions sanctify,
 All my words and thoughts receive;
Claim me for thy service, claim
All I have and all I am.

HLS, 129

All day long God is at work for good in the world. How are you partnering with God right now in that important work leading to shalom?

Serving Christ Alongside the Poor

At this season we usually distribute coals and bread among the poor. But I now considered they wanted clothes as well as food. So on this and the four following days I walked through the town and begged two hundred pounds in order to clothe those who wanted it most.

Works 23:340

Just as the love of God naturally leads to works of piety, so the love of our neighbor naturally leads all that feel it to works of mercy. It inclines us to feed the hungry, to clothe the naked, to visit them that are sick or in prison, to be as eyes to the blind, and feet to the lame, a husband to the widow, a father to the fatherless.

Works 3:191

The poor as Jesus' bosom friends,
 The poor he makes his latest care,
To all his followers commends,
 And wills us on our hands to bear;
The poor our dearest care we make,
 And love them for our Savior's sake.

MS Acts, 421

Do you ask how you shall improve them to the glory of the Giver? And are you willing to know? Then I will tell you how. Go and see the poor and sick in their own poor little hovels. Take up your cross, woman! Remember the faith! Jesus went before you and will go with you. Put off the gentlewoman. You bear a higher character.

Letters (Telford), 6:153

Mercy that heaven-descending guest,
Resided in her gentle breast,
 And full possession kept;
While listening to the orphan's moan,
And echoing back the widow's groan,
 She wept with them that wept.

A nursing mother to the poor,
For them she husbanded her store,
  Her life, her all, bestowed;
For them she labored day and night,
In doing good her whole delight,
  In copying after God.

Funeral Hymns, 52-53

O that God would enable me, before I leave this world, to lift up my voice like a trumpet to those who gain and save all they can but do not give all they can. Many of your brothers and sisters, beloved of God, have no food to eat. They have no clothes to put on. They have no place to lay their heads. Why are they so distressed? Because you impiously, unjustly, and cruelly hold onto what your Master puts in your hands for the purpose of supplying their wants! See that poor sister or brother pinched with hunger, shivering with cold, half naked! Meantime you have plenty of this world's goods, of food and clothing. In the name of God, what are you doing?

Works 4:91-92

**Reflect upon or discuss activities in which
you are involved alongside the poor. How
are these shaping your life of love?**

Doing Justice

The golden rule she has pursued,
And did to others as she would
  Others should do to her;

Justice composed her upright soul,
Justice did all her thoughts control,
    And formed her character.

Funeral Hymns, 51.

    But may not women as well as men use their gifts in ministry? Undoubtedly, they may! No, they must! It is proper, right, and their obligation. Does scripture not tell us that "there is neither male and female, for you are all one in Christ Jesus" (Galatians 3:28). Indeed, it has long passed as a maxim with many that women are to be seen and not heard. And accordingly, many of them are brought up in such a manner as if they were only designed for agreeable playthings! But is this doing honor to them or to God? Or is it a real kindness to them? No! It is the deepest unkindness. It is horrid cruelty. I know not how any woman of sense and spirit can submit to it. Let all you that have it in your power assert the right which God has given you. Yield not to that vile bondage any longer! You too are called of God!

Works 3:395-96

> **Identity several areas of injustice in our world today (and don't forget about your own community)! How are you involved in acts of justice or what are ways in which you can get involved?**

Waging Peace

    Beware of despising your opponents! Beware of anger and resentment! Never return evil for evil, or railing for railing. Never respond to attacks or the assaults of others with violence. To live peaceably with all people is the earnest desire of your affection brother. John Wesley

Letters (Telford), 6:228

There is war in the world! War between nations! War between Christians! I mean, between those that bear the name of Christ and profess to walk as he also walked. Now, who can reconcile war, I will not say to religion, but to any degree of reason or common sense? Whatever is the cause, let us calmly and impartially consider the thing itself. Here are forty thousand soldiers gathered together on this plain. What are they going to do? See, there are thirty or forty thousand more at a little distance. And these are going to shoot them through the head or body, to stab them, or split their skulls, and send them to their death. Why? What harm have they done to them? None at all! They do not so much as know them. But someone in leadership has a quarrel with another leader. So they will each kill as many of their opponents as they can. What an insane way of resolving conflict is this!

Works (Jackson), 9:221-22

Prince of universal peace,
  Destroy the enmity,
Bid our jars and discords cease,
  Unite us all in thee.
Cruel as wild beasts we are,
'Till vanquished by thy mercy's power,

We, like wolves, each other tear,
    And their own flesh devour.

But if thou pronounce the word
    That forms our souls again,
Love and harmony restored
    Throughout the earth shall reign;
When thy wondrous love they feel,
The human savages are tame,
    Ravenous wolves, and leopards dwell
    And stable with the lamb.

                      Scripture Hymns, 1:316

**Peace flows from a "heart of peace." What are
you doing to become a more "peace-filled"
human being and how do activities related to
peace work shape that peace in your heart?**

THOUGHTS ON THE PRESENT
SCARCITY OF PROVISIONS

1. Many studies have been conducted on the widespread problem of hunger. One expert insists that the current food shortage is due to one particular cause. Another assigns the blame to one or two more. Few seem to be interested, however, in viewing the problem as a whole. No one is addressing the root causes of hunger and the way in which they are interrelated in our society.

The Fact of Hunger

2. First we must ask, why are thousands of people starving, perishing for want in every part of the nation? The fact I know. I have seen it with my eyes in every corner of the land. I have known those who could only afford to eat a little coarse food once every other day.

3. I have known one in London (and one that a few years before had all the conveniences of life) picking up stinking fish from a dunghill and carrying them home for herself and her children. Such is the case right now for so many people in a land flowing, as it were, with milk and honey! Abounding with all the necessities, the conveniences, the superfluous luxuries of life!

The Causes of Hunger

4. Why is this? Why are so many starving before our very eyes? First of all, the main reason flour is so expensive is because such immense quantities of grain are continually consumed by distilling. Instead of being used for bread, it is used to produce gin. Indeed, a little less than half the wheat produced in the kingdom is consumed every year, not by so harmless a way as throwing it into the sea, but by converting it into deadly poison. This poison destroys not only the strength and life, but also the morals of our nation!

5. Another cause of hunger and poverty is luxury. What can stand against this? Will it not waste and destroy all that human ingenuity can produce? Only look into the kitchens of the rich. When you have observed the amazing waste which is made there, you will no longer wonder why others suffer. Gentlemen cannot maintain their standard of living without increasing their income. So they raise their rents. The farmer, paying a higher rent for his

land, must receive a higher price for his produce. And so the wheel turns round.

6. Another reason for our present situation is the enormous burden of taxes. But why are the taxes so high? Because of the national debt. Until the debt is discharged, the taxes must remain high. I have heard that the national expense, seventy years ago during a time of peace, was three million pounds a year. And now, the bare interest on the public debt amounts to above four million pounds annually! So long as the government maintains its current level of expense, those taxes are absolutely necessary.

7. To sum up the whole: thousands of people are starving to death because they do not have food. This is due to a number of causes, but primary among them are distilling, taxes, and luxury. Here are the evil and the undeniable causes of it. But where is the remedy?

What are you doing in your own community to alleviate hunger and poverty?

Striking at the Root of the Problem

8. The price of wheat, and therefore of bread, can be reduced by prohibiting distilling. Not only does this industry rob innocent children of the staff of life, it is the bane of health. It destroys strength and life and virtue. The repression of luxury would also help the hungry. Whether by laws, by example, or by both, the rich must see that their luxury is purchased at the expense of the poor! Taxes must be reduced and foolish expenses eliminated in the government in order to help the poor. A million pounds could be saved each year by abolishing useless spending by the Governors of forts and castles.

9. But will this ever be done? I fear not. What good can we expect for such a nation as this, where there is no fear of God. It seems as if God must surely arise and maintain the case of justice by divine means. If so, let us fall into the hands of God and not into the hands of God's faithless children.

Works (Jackson), 11:53-59

How does our silence or our unthinking participation in unjust aspects of our culture and society perpetuate injustice? How do we educate ourselves to make sure we are not contributing to unjust systems rather than solving problems related to justice?

THOUGHTS UPON SLAVERY

1. The main argument for the oppressors is that slavery is authorized by law. But can human law change the justice of God's created order? Can it turn darkness into light, or evil into good? By no means! Right is right, and wrong is still wrong. There is still an essential difference between justice and injustice, cruelty and mercy. And slavery cannot be reconciled either with mercy or justice!

Exposing Injustice

2. Is it just to inflict the severest evils on those who have done no wrong? Is it right to tear people away from their native home and deprive them of liberty? An African cherished freedom and possesses

it as a natural right as well as any European. Where is the justice in killing innocent, inoffensive people; murdering thousands of them in their own land; many thousands, year after year, on shipboard, and casting them like dung into the sea; and tens of thousands in that cruel slavery to which they are so unjustly reduced? I strike directly at the root of this complicated villainy. I absolutely deny that slavery can be reconciled with any degree of natural justice.

3. Slavery is also utterly inconsistent with mercy. This is too plain to even require proof. Some slave traders have argued that they subject Africans to slavery in order to save them from miserable lives or even death. Was it to save them from death that they knocked out the brains of those they could not bring away? They know their own conscience, if they have any conscience left. To make the matter short: Can thy say before God that they ever took a single voyage, or bought a single slave, from this motive? They cannot. They know all too well that the only motive of their actions was to get money, and not to save lives!

4. Even though slavery is inconsistent both with mercy and justice, some argue that it is simply necessary. "Damn justice" is their short and plain reply. "Slavery is necessary." You stumble from our first step. I deny that any villainy is ever necessary. It is impossible that it should ever be necessary for any reasonable creature to violate all the laws of justice, mercy, and truth. No circumstance can make it necessary for any person to tear apart all the ties of humanity! It can never be necessary for a rational being to sink below a brute! The absurdity of the assumption is so glaring, I wonder how any can fail to see it.

5. For those who argue that slaves are required for the cultivation of new frontiers, my response is plain. It would be better to sink those new lands to the depth of the sea than to develop them at so high a price as the violation of justice, mercy, and truth. For those

who argue for the trade, wealth, and glory of our nation, listen to me. Wealth is not necessary to the glory of any nation. But wisdom, virtue, justice, mercy, generosity, true patriotism, and love of country are. Better no trade than trade procured by villainy. It is far better to be penniless than to become rich at the expense of virtue. Honest poverty is of much greater value than riches bought by the tears, and sweat, and blood of our fellow human beings.

**What areas of injustice in our world
and our communities do we need to
expose? How do we do that?**

Advocacy for the Oppressed

6. How shall we bring an end to this misery? Should we address ourselves to the general public? This would only inflame the world against the guilty but is not likely to remove the guilt. Should we appeal to the nation? This is also sticking too wide and will probably not bring an end to the evil. It is only the oppressors themselves who can end this reign of terror. And so, I add a few words to those who are immediately concerned, whether captains, merchants, or planters.

7. May I speak plainly to you? I must. Love constrains me; love to you, as well as to those you are concerned with. Is there a God? You know there is. Is God just? If so, there must be a state of retribution, a state wherein God rewards people according to their works. What reward will God render you? O think about this carefully before you drop into eternity! What if God should deal with you as you have dealt with your African brothers and sisters?

8. Are you a human being? Then you should have a human heart. But do you have one? What is your heart made of? Is there no such principle as compassion there? Do you never feel another's pain? Have you no sympathy, no sense of human woe, no pity for the miserable? When you saw the tear-filled eyes, the heaving breasts, or the bleeding sides and tortured limbs of your fellow human beings, was your heart a stone? Have you degenerated to a brute? When you squeezed the agonizing creatures down in the ship, or when you threw their poor remains into the sea, did you feel nothing? Did not one tear drop from your eye? The great God will surely deal with you and require all of their blood at your hands.

9. But if your heart does relent, though in a small degree, know it is a call from the God of love. And today, if you will hear God's voice, don't harden your heart. Today resolve, God being your helper, to escape for your life. Do not make money your god! Whatever you lose, don't lose your soul. Quit this horrid crime immediately and become an honest human being. Give liberty to whom liberty is due, that is to every child of God. Away with all whips, all chains, all compulsion! Be gentle toward all people. See that you invariably do unto everyone as you would have them do unto you.

Works (Jackson), 11:59-79

It is important for us to point out injustice and work to change unjust systems, but we also need to make our justice work personal. How can you reach out to those who are oppressed as allies and advocates in your own communities?

A Seasonable Address by
a Lover of Peace

1. Who would not do everything possible to prevent war? For who knows, when the sword is once drawn, where it will stop? Who can command it to be put back into its scabbard? It will not obey!

The Victims of War

2. The victims of war not only include the soldier, but the beloved spouse, an aged parent, a tender child, a dear relative. What can make up for such a loss? What, O! What would the whole world mean if it might be gained? Alas! What a poor trade! But suppose you escape with your life and the lives of those who are near and dear to you. There is another dreadful consequence: plunder and all the evil it entails. O brothers and sisters, can we not abandon war forever?

3. Stop and survey the desolation of war. Behold the weeping and disconsolate widow refusing to be comforted. Her beloved husband is fallen! Is fallen and she will never see him again! See the affectionate parents hanging down their heads! Hear the broken language of the mother's heart! "My son, my son, would to God I had died in his place! O my son, my son!" This is the real and actual condition of war. While we are biting and devouring one another, these stronger beasts of prey step in and divide the spoil!

4. What is war? Look! Here are some thousands of our brave countrymen gathered together on this plain. They are followed by the most tender and feeling emotions of spouses, children, and an innumerable multitude of their thoughtful, humane, and sympathizing countrymen. Then turn your eyes and behold a superior number

at a little distance who only a few years ago were friends. Likewise, they are loved and cared for by spouses, and children, and friends.

5. They advance towards each other, prepared with every instrument of death. But what are they going to do? To shoot each other through the head or heart; to stab and butcher each other, and each other towards death. So they murder each other with all possible haste to prove who is in the right. O, at what a price do we make such decisions!

We all see the images of war on our televisions and devices almost daily. It can seem overwhelming and as if there is nothing we can do. Explore our United Methodist Church and Society website and reflect on or talk about where you can get involved. GBCS Home • GBCS (umcjustice.org)

Nonviolent Conflict Resolution

6. Now, who that seriously considers this tragedy can help lamenting the astonishing lack of wisdom? Are there no wise people among us? Can no one resolve this conflict by any other means? Brother goes to war against brother. Surely this is an inexcusable evil! How are the mighty fallen! How is wisdom destroyed! What a flood of folly and madness has broken in upon us?

7. Reason seems lost in the screaming. Confusion of passion and position reign. The satanic dust of prejudice seems to have put out the eyes of our understanding. While we are contending who set the building on fire and looking with rage and vengeance on

the suspected party, the flames are spreading and threaten the entire building. Instead of bringing the water of heartfelt grief and sincere concern, with the helping hand of wisdom, moderation, and love, we consume ourselves in the flames of war.

8. Let us cease contending with each other. Let us avoid unkind and bitter reflection on one another, seeing it can do no real service to the cause we would defend. Let us resolve not to bring combustible materials of this sort to increase the fire. Instead, let us do our utmost to extinguish the blaze. Jesus described the Christian family as the salt of the earth. Exert the seasoning, preserving quality with which you are favored. Bring your adversaries into your loving arms of faith and prayer. Remember them earnestly before the God who loves you both.

9. Let no Christian engage in the controversy in the spirit and temper of the world. Do not bite and devour one another unless you wish to be consumed with the world. Rather, let your mind be that of the prophet: "If only my head were a spring of water, and my eyes a fountain of tears, I would weep day and night for the wounds of my people" (Jeremiah 9:1). There could be no more admirable way of showing our love for our country! We could find no better service!

10. The bible gives a clear account of the rise and fall of empires. They rose by virtue; they fell by vice. Righteousness alone exalts a nation, but sin is a reproach to all people. And this will always be the case, even to the end of all things. What peace can we expect, therefore, so long as we participate in such evil? As long as we follow this course, we are doomed to destroy ourselves. Repentance is the first and principal means of restoring the peace we all desire. Reconciliation comes as we accept the friendship of God. If we remember

our own brokenness and failure, and not that of our neighbor, God's power to reconcile will be at work among us. If the Prince of Peace is with us, who can be against us?

Works (Jackson), 11:119-28

Conflict is unavoidable. But how do we deal with it? That is the question. Reflect on or discuss a situation that you helped deescalate so that violence of heart or action could be averted.

The Character of a Methodist: A Portrait of Love

A Concluding Exhortation

Christlikeness is the ultimate goal for the believer and for the community of faith. You have now immersed yourself in what this means for someone in the Wesleyan tradition. In this process of spiritual growth, the Spirit restores the image of Christ in our lives and conforms our communities into his likeness as well. God calls us into peace, into freedom, and into a life of loving and joyful service.

Perhaps this study has illuminated an unexplored area in your own pilgrimage with Christ. It may have helped you and conversation partners in the journey rediscover something about church that you are now excited to live into more fully. Celebrate the discoveries you have made about yourself and your community of faith. God has probably awakened a gift, a new relationship, a unique ministry, and exciting area of mission. Remember that Christ is the power and wisdom of God to those who are called.

We hope that this is only the beginning of a wonderful adventure. The dimensions of your life in and with God are boundless. Your true calling in life is to love as you have been loved by God in Christ. There is no limit to the ways in which that love can be expressed in your life through loving witness and service. Continue to explore. Allow the Living Word to form and transform your life and that of your church. Wait for God in the means of grace where we meet Christ.

Christlikeness is both a gift and a goal. While intensely personal, it is impotent apart from the community of faith. We participate together in a glorious drama—the embodiment of God's vision of wholeness for your life and the life of the world. This quest for shalom involves much struggle, but it is also the source of our greatest hope. It is only when you risk embracing life's tensions and challenges that your pilgrimage with Christ will become an adventure filled with hope. As Methodists, we are all in connection with one another, bound together in a journey of faith working by love leading to holiness of heart and life.

<hr>

THE CHARACTER OF A METHODIST

1. Since the name first came into popular use, many have been at a loss to know exactly what it means to be a Methodist. What are the principles and practices that characterize the life of such a disciple? What are the distinguishing marks of this group which is spoken against everywhere? The "Methodists" did not choose this title for themselves; rather, it was used originally to ridicule their disciplined

life of faith. Even though some may still hate what we are called, perhaps they may learn to love what we are by the grace of God.

2. Methodists are not distinguished by their opinions. We believe that all scripture is inspired by God. We believe that the Bible is the only and sufficient rule both of faith and of practice. We believe Christ to be the eternal, supreme God. But with regard to opinions that do not strike at the root of Christianity, we think and let think.

3. Neither is our religion, or any part of it, to be reduced to the way we talk about God or faith—reduced, that is, to doctrine. Our living faith is not to be found in any peculiar way of speaking or any set uncommon expressions. Language can only reflect a small part of the fullness and variety of divine love. It is a terrible mistake, therefore, to identify Methodists simply by their words or doctrines. In fact, we don't want to be characterized by any human symbols, whether they are words, actions, customs, or peculiar traditions.

4. The Methodists, likewise, are not set apart by their emphasis on any one part of the whole of religion. If you say simply that a Methodist believes we are saved by faith alone, you do not understand the fullness of the terms. Salvation for the Methodist is love filling the heart and life. And all Methodists affirm that this goal of the Christ life is the consequence of true faith alone. Faith and love, grace and holiness must never be separated. The fullness of life in Christ cannot be reduced to either doing no harm, or doing good constantly, or participating in the means of grace. True religion, according to the Methodists, is faith working by love leading to holiness.

5. Who then are the Methodists? Methodists are those disciples of Christ who have the love of God poured into their hearts by

means of the Holy SprIit. They love God with all their heart, with all their soul, with all their mind, and with all their strength. God is the joy of their hearts and the desire of their souls. They constantly cry out, "Whom have I in heaven but you? There is nothing I desire but you! My God and my all! You are the strength of my heart and my portion forever!"

6. Methodists are happy in God. Having found salvation through Christ, and forgiveness for all their sins, they cannot help rejoicing. They rejoice now because God has given the gift of a new relationship to them in Christ. Through him they have found peace with God and they rejoice whenever they look to the future because of their hope in the glory they have been promised in him.

7. They have learned to be content in their life. They know what it means to be humble and how to live with plenty. Everywhere, and in all things, they are instructed both to be full and to be hungry. They pray without ceasing. Not that they are always in church on their knees, but the language of their hearts is:

> Thou brightness of the eternal glory,
> Unto thee is my heart,
> Though without a voice,
> And my silence speaketh unto thee.

8. This commandment is written upon their hearts: Whoever desires to love God must love neighbor! And so, they love their brothers and sisters in the world as they love themselves. Their hearts are full of love to all humankind. This is their one desire because it is the will of God. Their one intention is to love as they have been loved.

9. Their obedience to God's will, therefore, is in proportion to God's love, the source from which it flows. Loving God with all their

heart, they serve God with all their strength. They present their souls and bodies as living sacrifices, holy and acceptable to God. They entirely and without reserve devote themselves, all they have and all they are, to the glory of God.

10. Not only is this their intention, but they are able to attain it by the power of God's grace. Their one invariable rule is this: Whatever you do, in word or in deed, do it all in the name of the Lord Jesus, giving thanks to God through him. Nothing in the world can hinder them from running the race that is set before them.

11. They cannot overeat while others go hungry. They cannot store up riches for themselves here on earth. They cannot waste their money on expensive clothes. They cannot join in or countenance any amusements that are unsuitable. They cannot speak evil of their neighbors. Love keeps the door of their lips. But whatever is pure, whatever is lovely, whatever is just, they think, and speak, and act, adoring the gospel of our Lord Jesus Christ in all things.

12. Finally, as they have time, they do good to all people. They feed the hungry. They provide clothing for the needy. They visit the sick. They go to prisons and try to bring light to the lost. Not only do they attend to these physical needs that they see all around them, but they offer Christ to God's children wherever they go. Only God through the grace of our Lord, Jesus Christ, can enable them to do these things.

13. These then are the principles and practices of our community. These are the marks of a true Methodist. If you say, "Why, these are only the common fundamental principles of Christianity" this is the very truth. I know they are no other and I would to God that both you and all other people knew how we refuse to be distinguished from any other group but by the common principles of

our faith. All I teach is the plain, old Christianity, renouncing and detesting all other marks of distinction.

14. Whoever conforms to what I preach (let them be called what they will, for names change nothing in the nature of the thing), is a Christian. That person is a Christian not in name only, but in heart and life. This is what it means to be a Christian and a Methodist:

> To be inwardly and outwardly conformed to God's will as
> revealed in scripture;
> To think, speak, and live according to the method laid down
> by Jesus Christ;
> To be renewed in the image of God, so as to walk even as
> Christ also walked.

15. By these marks, by these fruits of a living faith, we seek to distinguish ourselves from the unbelieving world. We wish to be disassociated from all those whose minds and lives are not conformed to the gospel of Christ. But from real Christians, regardless of their denomination, we have never desired to be separate at all. Do you love and serve God? Is it enough! I give you the right hand of fellowship.

Works 9:31-46

   To love is all my wish,
    I only live for this:
  Grant me, Lord, my heart's desire,
    There by faith forever dwell:
  This I always will require
    Thee and only thee to feel.

Thy power I pant to prove
Rooted and fixed in love,
Strengthened by thy Spirit's might,
Wise to fathom things divine,
What the length and breadth and height,
What the depth of love like thine.

HSP (1739), 169

Take a moment to reflect on or discuss this
study as a whole. What have you learned? What
practices have you taken up? How has it changed
your vision of the future church? What can you
now do to celebrate who you are as a United
Methodist and what you are called to do?

Sources

Catholic Love   Wesley, Charles. "Catholic Love."
Appended to John Wesley. Catholic Spirit.
London: Cock, 1755.

Christian Perfection   Wesley, John. *A Plain Account of Christian
Perfection*. Edited by Paul W. Chilcote and
Randy L. Maddox. Kansas City: Beacon
Hill Press, 2015.

CW Sermons   Wesley, Charles. *The Sermons of Charles
Wesley: A Critical Edition with Introduc-
tion and Notes*. Edited by Kenneth G.
C. Newport. Oxford: Oxford University
Press, 2002.

Funeral Hymns   Wesley, Charles. *Funeral Hymns*. London:
Strahan, 1759.

HLS   Wesley, Charles. *Hymns for the Nativity of
our Lord*. London: Strahan, 1745.

HSP (1739)   Wesley, John and Charles. *Hymns and
Sacred Poems*. London: Strahan, 1739.

HSP (1740)	Wesley, John and Charles. *Hymns on the Lord's Supper*. Bristol: Farley, 1740.
HSP (1742)	Wesley, John and Charles. *Hymns and Sacred Poems*. Bristol: Farley, 1742.
HSP (1749)	Wesley, Charles. *Hymns and Sacred Poems*. 2 vols. Bristol: Farley, 1749.
Letters (Telford)	Wesley, John. *The Letters of the Rev. John Wesley, A.M.* Edited by John Telford. 8 vols. London: The Epworth Press, 1931.
MS Acts	Wesley, Charles. Manuscript Hymns on the Acts of the Apostles.
Redemption Hymns	Wesley, Charles. *Hymns for Those that Seek and Those that have Redemption in the Blood of Jesus Christ*. London: Strahan, 1747.
Scripture Hymns	Wesley, Charles. *Short Hymns on Select Passages of the Holy Scriptures*. 2 vols. Bristol: Farley, 1762.
UMH	The United Methodist Hymnal. Nashville: The United Methodist Publishing House, 1989.
Works 1	Wesley, John. *The Works of John Wesley. Volume 1. Sermons I, 1-33*. Edited by Albert C. Outler. Nashville: Abingdon Press, 1984.
Works 2	Wesley, John. *The Works of John Wesley. Volume 2. Sermons II, 34-70*. Edited by Albert C. Outler. Nashville: Abingdon Press, 1985.

Works 3   Wesley, John. *The Works of John Wesley.*
               Volume 3. Sermons III, 71-114. Edited by
               Albert C. Outler. Nashville: Abingdon
               Press, 1986.

Works 4   Wesley, John. *The Works of John Wesley.*
               Volume 4. Sermons IV, 115-51. Edited by
               Albert C. Outler. Nashville: Abingdon
               Press, 1987.

Works 9   Wesley, John. *The Works of John Wesley.*
               Volume 9. The Methodist Societies: History,
               Nature, and Design. Edited by Rupert E.
               Davies. Nashville: Abingdon Press, 1989.

Works 11   Wesley, John. *The Works of John Wesley.*
               Volume 11. The Appeals to Men of Reason
               and Religion. Edited by Gerald R. Cragg.
               Oxford: Clarendon Press, 1975.

Works 19   Wesley, John. *The Works of John Wesley,*
               Volume 19, Journals and Diaries II (1738-
               1743). Edited by W. Reginald Ward and
               Richard P. Heitzenrater. Nashville: Abing-
               don Press, 1990.

Works 23   Wesley, John. *The Works of John Wesley,*
               Volume 19, Journals and Diaries VI (1776-
               1786). Edited by W. Reginald Ward and
               Richard P. Heitzenrater. Nashville: Abing-
               don Press, 1995.

Works 25   Wesley, John. *The Works of John Wesley.*
               Volume 25. Letters I, 1721-1739. Edited

	by Frank Baker. Nashville: Abingdon Press, 1980.
Works 27	Wesley, John. *The Works of John Wesley. Volume 27. Letters III, 1756-1765.* Edited by Ted A. Campbell. Nashville: Abingdon Press, 2015.
Works (Jackson)	Wesley, John. *The Works of John Wesley.* Edited by Thomas Jackson. 14 vols. Reprint Edition. Grand Rapids: Zondervan, 1958.

Printed in the USA
CPSIA information can be obtained
at www.ICGtesting.com
LVHW032142120424
777043LV00002B/5